THE STORIES OF KRISHNA

PART II

The Editors wish to acknowledge the role played by David Stollar and other members of the St James School Sanskrit faculty in the preparation of the material for the Sanskrit Course.

The Stories of Krishna

A Sanskrit Coursebook For Beginners

Edited by
WARWICK JESSUP
ELENA JESSUP

PART II

MOTILAL BANARSIDASS PUBLISHERS
PRIVATE LIMITED • DELHI

Reprint : Delhi, 2016
First Indian Edition : Delhi, 2012
First Edition: London, 1997 (2001, 2005)

Published under arrangements with
St. James School,
Sanskrit Department, London

ISBN : 978-81-208-3548-1 (PB Part I)
ISBN : 978-81-208-3549-8 (PB Part II)

MOTILAL BANARSIDASS
41 U.A. Bungalow Road, Jawahar Nagar, Delhi 110 007
8 Mahalaxmi Chamber, 22 Bhulabhai Desai Road, Mumbai 400 026
203 Royapettah High Road, Mylapore, Chennai 600 004
236, 9th Main III Block, Jayanagar, Bengaluru 560 011
8 Camac Street, Kolkata 700 017
Ashok Rajpath, Patna 800 004
Chowk, Varanasi 221 001

Printed using Times, Marking-RomanTM (transliteration) and SanskritpadaTM fonts designed and distributed by 6H Software, London (Tel. 020-8944 9496); © 1993-4 6H Software.

COVER DRAWING: Kṛṣṇa playing his flute

Printed in India

by RP Jain at NAB Printing Unit,
A-44, Naraina Industrial Area, Phase I, New Delhi–110028
and published by JP Jain for Motilal Banarsidass Publishers (P) Ltd.,
41 U.A. Bungalow Road, Jawahar Nagar, Delhi-110007

Foreword

by Prof Dr Satya Vrat Shastri

After a thorough perusal of these text books written by teachers of St James Schools in London for the teaching of Sanskrit, I am convinced of their utility for Indian schools. They are well-graded and supported by appropriate illustrations that make them very attractive to learners, particularly the young.

Today many Indian universities offer Sanskrit as an optional subject, even for those who are majoring in other subjects. For these students the books would be very effective in introducing them to Sanskrit which they might not have studied previously. The books could also be useful for those involved in performing arts like dance and music, or for students of Yoga and Ayurveda, subjects which have many Sanskrit references.

The first group of books entitled Sanskrit is Fun (3 volumes) introduce the learners to the Devanagari alphabet grouping the letters according to their place of articulation. Each group is given a designation, 'Family'. The 'Family' comprises both the vowels and the consonants. The learners are first taught how to draw the letters. The teaching is also helped by the humorous presentation of them in the form of animal figures. The next step is to add vowels to the consonants and then to teach joint consonants. Finally words and sentences are formed.

The second group of books seek to teach Sanskrit with reference to age-old stories of Krishna (2 volumes) and Rama (2 volumes). These stories with perennial interest of their own are then pressed into service to teach vocabulary, the formation of nouns and the conjugation of verbs in all three tenses. Adjectives and prepositions are also covered .

By the time learners have completed these books it is expected they would have a good basic grasp of the Sanskrit language, its vocabulary, structure and grammar. These books are an attempt to teach Sanskrit in a simple and systematic way that may well dispel the notion that Sanskrit is a difficult language.

Dr Shastri is currently an Honorary Professor at the Special Centre for Sanskrit Studies, Jawaharlal Nehru University, New Delhi. He was the Head of the Department of Sanskrit and the Dean of the Faculty of Arts at the University of Delhi, where he was the Pandit Manmohan Nath Dar Professor of Sanskrit (1970–1995).

Contents – Part Two

Preface

by Professor Richard Gombrich

It is a privilege for me to be invited to introduce this set of textbooks. They have been compiled with loving care by the teachers of the Sanskrit Department of St James School in London. Their slow birth reflects the years of teaching experience which have gone into their making.

Sanskrit is by no means an easy language: even in India it is mastered only by a small minority of the population. The grammar is complicated, even if someone who masters it will finally discover that it is more systematic and less irregular than that of English. The vocabulary is vast, reflecting the vast span of time and geographical area over which Sanskrit has been used. Learning to read and write an Indian script is also a major undertaking for a student from another culture. (Luckily for us Europeans, at least it is written left to write and top to bottom.)

On the other hand, Sanskrit is not only a beautiful language written in a beautiful script; it is the vehicle of classical Indian culture, the culture which has given the world one of its greatest literatures and greatest civilizations. Sanskrit achieved something not very different from the form it still has today more than three thousand years ago. The reason why it has survived so well, and may well outlive most of the languages which the world is now using, is not hard to understand: it is because of the aesthetic attractions and the intellectual and spiritual value of the content of so many Sanskrit texts.

Only a few students are likely to have the opportunity to go on to study Sanskrit in depth, so that they can enjoy reading Sanskrit by themselves. There will be so many rival claims on their attention. But even those who only work through these books are likely to look back on the experience with satisfaction, a feeling that they have done something truly worth while. And the few who go further will be grateful that these books have launched them on an unforgettable experience.

Prof Gombrich was the Boden Professor of Sanskrit at the University of Oxford from 1976 to 2004 and was a past President of the Pali Text Society (1994–2002) and General Editor Emeritus of the Clay Sanskrit Library. He is currently the Boden Professor of Sanskrit Emeritus, University of Oxford

Introduction to the Sanskrit Language

Language is fundamental to a human being. For this reason, it is a primary element in education. Language is one of the greatest gifts that a student is given. How a person learns to speak is all important and will be determined by example. So the aim of the teacher should be to present the student with the finest language.

Linguists agree that one of the finest languages is Sanskrit. Sir William Jones, recognised as a founder of modern linguistics, said in 1786:

> "The Sanskrit language, whatever be its antiquity, is of a wonderful structure; more perfect than the Greek, more copious than the Latin, and more exquisitely refined than either; yet bearing to both of them a stronger affinity, both in the roots of verbs and the forms of grammar, than can possibly have been produced by accident."

The considerable benefits of studying the classical languages, Greek and Latin, have been known in the West for hundreds of years; indeed, in recent centuries some of the best education available in the world has been based upon them. However, Sir William Jones had discovered a classical language *par excellence,* more ancient than Greek or Latin, which had been preserved intact for thousands of years.

The word 'Sanskrit' means 'perfected', for its sound system and grammar are scientifically structured. It has even been put forward as being the most suitable language for use in computers (see 'Knowledge Representation in Sanskrit and Artificial Intelligence', *The A.I. Magazine,* Spring 1985).

Sanskrit also has one of the greatest literatures known to humanity. The Sanskrit epics, the *Rāmāyaṇa* and the *Mahābhārata,* are inspiring and fascinating. Readers of all ages love these stories and enjoy the company of great and heroic men and women.

Notes for Teachers/Students

THE COURSE

This book forms the second part of the 'Stories of Krishna' and is suitable for students who have established an elementary grounding in Sankrit. Part One is aimed at students familiar with reading and writing the Sanskrit script, and covers:

- some of the basic parts of a sentence;
- the first four case-endings
- three stories based on the childhood of Krishna;
- practice for reading the script.

Part Two starts with a brief revision of main grammatical points covered in the first volume and then presents:

- the final three case-endings;
- an introduction to all the forms of a typical noun in each of the three genders;
- an introduction to all the forms of a typical verb in the present, future and past tenses;
- nine further stories based on the early life of Krishna.

This second volume leads on to a textbook of more advanced material based on the stories of Prince Rāma.

WRITING

Part Two, unlike the earlier volume, is ***not*** intended to be a workbook in which students write. They will need separate lined exercise books for this purpose. Where students are asked to copy words which, in the volume, are shown in grids, the gridlines themselves need not be copied.

STORIES

By the time the stories are reached in this book, a reader would do well to have familiarised him or herself with the tales of Krishna's childhood, around which the book is based. These will be found in the *Śrīmad Bhāgavatam*, available in many translations. Such familiarity will enable the reader to understand the story naturally and simply in the Sanskrit version. As with most situations, it is best not to read from a book but rather to speak from a well funded memory and the inspiration of the moment.

Before a new story is begun, the new words should be practised orally over the course of several lessons. Words which the reader has met before should also be practised again. Then he should practise one sentence at a time, reading and repeating the sentence carefully. He should then go for translation.

This process should be repeated over several sessions until the story is quite well known. A useful exercise at this stage is to read the story out with one word in each sentence left out. The reader should be able to give the sentence back with the word replaced. It is worth mentioning that these stories lend themselves to being acted out.

In writing translations of individual words the reader should include the preposition corresponding with the particular ending of the word (e.g., from Rāma, in the house, etc.). Since in English no preposition is used for the object, it being known by word order alone, he should add (2nd) after the English translation of the object of the sentence.

TEXTS FOR RECITATION

Appendix 1 to this volume comprises a small selection of suggested Sanskrit texts which students could recite on a daily basis. It has been found that this often enhances the students's experience of the beauty of the language and of its fluent pronunciation. The selection is, of course, only a sample of what can be found. Students may wish to add some of their favourite texts.

OTHER DETAILS

Regular practice of all the noun declensions and of the conjugations of verbs so far covered needs to continue as the course proceeds.

Key to Transliteration and Pronunciation

The English words given are only close equivalents to the Sanskrit and refer to what used to be called 'BBC English' pronunciation.

अ	a	as in	*approach*	ङ	ṅ	as in	*long*
आ	ā	as in	*star*	च	c	as in	*chalk*
इ	i	as in	*if*	छ	ch	as in	*catch him*
ई	ī	as in	*feel*	ज	j	as in	*jug*
उ	u	as in	*book*	झ	jh	as in	*hedgehog*
ऊ	ū	as in	*food*	ञ	ñ	as in	*cringe*
ऋ	ṛ	a sound made with the tip of the tongue raised but not quite touching the roof of the mouth		ट	ṭ	as in	*take**
				ठ	ṭh	as in	*anthill**
ए	e	as in	*say*	ड	ḍ	as in	*do**
ऐ	ai	as in	*my*	ढ	ḍh	as in	*godhood**
ओ	o	as in	*home*	ण	ṇ	as in	*under**
औ	au	as in	*now*	त	t	as in	*table*
क	k	as in	*kite*	थ	th	as in	*anthill*
ख	kh	as in	*blockhead*	द	d	as in	*day*
ग	g	as in	*gate*	ध	dh	as in	*god-head*
घ	gh	as in	*log-hut*	न	n	as in	*no*

[Continued on next page →]

[→ continued from preceding page]

प	p	as in	***pure***	व	v	as in	*awake*
फ	ph	as in	*loop-**h**ole*	श	ś	as in	***sh**all*
ब	b	as in	***b**aby*	ष	ṣ	as in	***sh**ow**
भ	bh	as in	*a**bh**or*	स	s	as in	***s**lug*
म	m	as in	***m**other*	ह	h	as in	***h**eaven*
य	y	as in	***y**ellow*	ं	ṁ	as in pure nasal	
र	r	as in	***r**osy**	ः	ḥ	as in a breath	
ल	l	as in	***l**ady*				

[* with the tip of the tongue raised to the roof of the mouth]

CHAPTER 1

What We Learnt in Part One

The class should be reminded of, and tested on, the following definitions, and should be asked to give examples of each.

- A **noun** is *a name*.
- An **adjective** tells *the quality of something*.
- A **verb** is *an action*.
- The **First Ending** shows *the doer*.
- The **Vocative Ending** shows *the person called*.
- The **Second Ending** shows *the thing done to*.
- The **Third Ending** shows *what an action is done by or with*.
- The **Fourth Ending** shows *what an action is done for*.

THE FORMS OF राम

Practise reciting the following forms of राम before moving on to Exercise 1.
The form रामम् should be translated as 'Rāma (2nd)'
in order to distinguish it from that of रामः.

So far we have learnt these five:

रामः	Rāma
हे राम	O Rāma
रामम्	Rāma (2nd)
रामेण	by Rāma
रामाय	for Rāma

Exercise 1

In your exercise book, write the answers to these questions.

1. नीलः खगः खादति।
   - **(a)** Which is the verb ?
   - **(b)** Which is the noun ?
   - **(c)** Which is the adjective ?
   - **(d)** Translate the sentence.

2. हे कृष्ण गजः गृहम् गच्छति।
   - **(a)** Which is the verb ?
   - **(b)** Which word has the Vocative Ending ?
   - **(c)** Which word has the First Ending ?
   - **(d)** Translate the sentence.

3. नरः प्राज्ञाय कृष्णाय नमति।
   - **(a)** Which is the verb ?
   - **(b)** Which word has the First Ending ?
   - **(c)** Which word has the Fourth Ending ?
   - **(d)** Translate the sentence.

4. हे नर प्रबलः भीमः हस्तेन फलम् खादति।

(a) Which is the verb ?

(b) Which word has the Vocative Ending ?

(c) Which word has the First Ending ?

(d) Which word has the Third Ending ?

(e) Which is the adjective ?

(f) Translate the sentence.

5. * SPECIAL BONUS QUESTION * Where has the verb come in each of the Sanskrit sentences above? At the beginning, middle or end of the sentence?

CHAPTER 2

The Fifth Ending

A noun can show where the action comes ***from***.

- The man walks ***from*** **the town.**
- The fruit falls ***from*** **the tree.**
- Wisdom comes ***from*** **the teacher.**

Exercise 2

Copy these sentences into your exercise book, and underline in ORANGE where these actions come *from*.

1. The girl comes from the forest.
2. The sword falls from his hand.
3. The enemy runs away from the battle.
4. Trouble comes from laziness.
5. The astronaut travels from the moon.

In Sanskrit,
to say where an
action comes **from**
we use a special
ending.

This is the
Fifth Ending.

The Fifth
Ending
means
'from'.

Exercise 3

Copy these sentences into your exercise book, and underline in ORANGE the words which would take the Fifth Ending in Sanskrit.

1. O king, the soldier is arriving by horse from the city.

2. The girl goes from home to school by foot.

3. Peace comes from wisdom, O noble prince.

4. Bhīma runs from his wife to the terrible battle.

5. The boy picks a fruit from the tree for his mother.

The Fifth Ending is –आत्.

So

रामः becomes रामात् 'from Rāma'

and

गजः becomes गजात् 'from an elephant'.

Exercise 4

Here are some words with First Endings. Opposite these are given the same words but with Fifth Endings. Copy all the following words into your exercise book, and say what they mean underneath. The first one is done for you.

हस्तः	हस्तात्
hand	from the hand

सिंहः	सिंहात्
मत्स्यः	मत्स्यात्

Exercise 5

In your exercise book first copy the following words, starting a new line for each word. Then beside them write the same words with Fifth Endings. Finally write the English meanings of the words which have the Fifth Endings.

For example:

खगः खगात् 'from a bird'

1. रथः
2. गजः
3. सिंहः
4. वंशः
5. हस्तः

THE FORMS OF राम

Practise reciting the following forms of राम before moving on to Exercise 6.
The form रामम् should be translated as 'Rāma (2nd)'
in order to distinguish it from that of रामः.

So far we have learnt these six:

रामः	Rāma
हे राम	O Rāma
रामम्	Rāma (2nd)
रामेण	by Rāma
रामाय	for Rāma
रामात्	from Rāma

Exercise 6

For each of the following sentences:

(a) Copy it beautifully into your exercise book.

(b) Write a translation below each word.

(c) Give a full translation of the sentence.

For example:

कुक्कुरः	सिंहात्	धावति ।
dog	from lion	runs

'The dog runs from the lion.'

1. सर्पः कुक्कुरात् धावति ।
2. खगः वृक्षात् गच्छति ।
3. रामः हस्तात् पिबति ।
4. नरः रथात् पतति ।
5. राक्षसः कृष्णात् धावति ।

NEW WORDS:

आगच्छति comes　　प्लवनम् a jump

करोति makes

[The following exercise is for faster pupils only.]

Exercise 7

➤ Remember सः 'he' and सा 'she'.

➤ Note: In Sanskrit, the verb comes at the end of a sentence, as in

रामः　सर्पम्　पश्यति।

Rāma　snake (2nd)　sees

Rāma sees a snake.

Copy the following English sentences. For each give a Sanskrit word-for-word translation, and then give a translation with correct Sanskrit word order.

For example:

He	falls	from the elephant.
सः	पतति	गजात्।

सः गजात् पतति।

1. She runs from the snake.
2. The man comes from the chariot.
3. Kṛṣṇa sees the lion.
4. He makes a jump.

[Once the new words are well known, the students should, without looking at the text, repeat each sentence after the teacher and then volunteer a translation. This should be repeated over several lessons. See the Notes for Teachers/Students on page xii. Students working alone should adapt these practices according to their available resources.]

STORY 1

Kṛṣṇa Overcomes the Serpent Demon

NEW WORDS:

नदी river	कालियः Kāliya, the serpent demon
आरोहति climbs	तुदति hits
तत्र there	जयति conquers
प्रविशति enters	
विषम् poison	

1. कृष्णः गृहात् नदीम् गच्छति।

2. जलात् विषम् आगच्छति।

3. कृष्णः वृक्षम् आरोहति।

(continues on page 18 →)

Kṛṣṇa overcomes Kāliya.

(continued from page 16)

4. वृक्षात् कृष्णः प्लवनम् करोति।

5. सः जलम् प्रविशति।

6. तत्र सर्पः अस्ति।

7. सर्पः राक्षसः अस्ति।

8. विषम् सर्पात् आगच्छति।

9. कृष्णः कालियम् तुदति।

10. सः कालियम् जयति।

11. कालियः कृष्णाय नमति॥

[The teacher should find this story on page 109 of Volume 3 of the 'Śrīmad Bhāgavatam', translated by Swami Tapasyananda (1981), and fill in the details for the class.]

CHAPTER 3

The Sixth Ending

A noun can show who has something. In English we say ***of***.

- The smile ***of*** **the lady**
- The wisdom ***of*** **the teacher**
- The king ***of*** **the country**

Exercise 8

Copy the following into your exercise book, and underline in BLACK ***who*** or ***what*** has something.

1. the flowers of the girl

2. the trees of the forest

3. the chariots of the enemy

4. the fearlessness of the boy

5. the courage of the astronaut

In Sanskrit,
to say who ***has***
something we use a
special ending.

This is the
Sixth Ending.

The Sixth
Ending
means
'of'.

Exercise 9

Copy these sentences into your exercise book, and underline in BLACK the words which would take the Sixth Ending in Sanskrit.

1. The cat of the girl caught a mouse.

2. The teacher marks the book of the pupil.

3. The prince ruled the people of the city for many years.

4. The soldiers of the king showed their courage in the battle.

5. Kṛṣṇa is the friend of the cowherdesses.

The Sixth Ending is –स्य.

So

रामः becomes रामस्य 'of Rāma'

and

गजः becomes गजस्य 'of an elephant'.

Exercise 10

Read the three examples in the shaded box below and then copy them into your exercise book.

Examples:

खगः	खगस्य	of a bird
रामः	रामस्य	of Rāma
गजः	गजस्य	of an elephant

Exercise 11

(a) Copy into your exercise book, one below the other, the six words given below. They all have First Endings.

(b) Now write next to them the same words but with Sixth Endings.

(c) Finally, alongside each word with a Sixth Ending, give the English meaning. The first is done for you.

1. रथः   रथस्य   of the chariot

2. गजः

3. रामः

4. सिंहः

5. कृष्णः

6. राक्षसः

Exercise 12

In your exercise book, copy these sentences and then give an English translation for each.

For example: कृष्णस्य वंशः the flute of Kṛṣṇa

1. सिंहस्य आस्यम्
2. नरस्य रथः
3. गृहस्य द्वारम्
4. सर्पस्य विषम्
5. नरस्य हृदयम्
6. भीमस्य नासिका
7. कुक्कुरस्य जलम्
8. रामस्य चिबुकम्

For "the flute of Kṛṣṇa"
we can say "Kṛṣṇa's flute".
Now, write out your answers again
in this new way.

THE FORMS OF राम

Practise reciting the following forms of राम
before moving on.

So far we have learnt these seven:

रामः	Rāma
हे राम	O Rāma
रामम्	Rāma (2nd)
रामेण	by Rāma
रामाय	for Rāma
रामात्	from Rāma
रामस्य	of Rāma

THE 'WHOSE IS IT ?' GAME

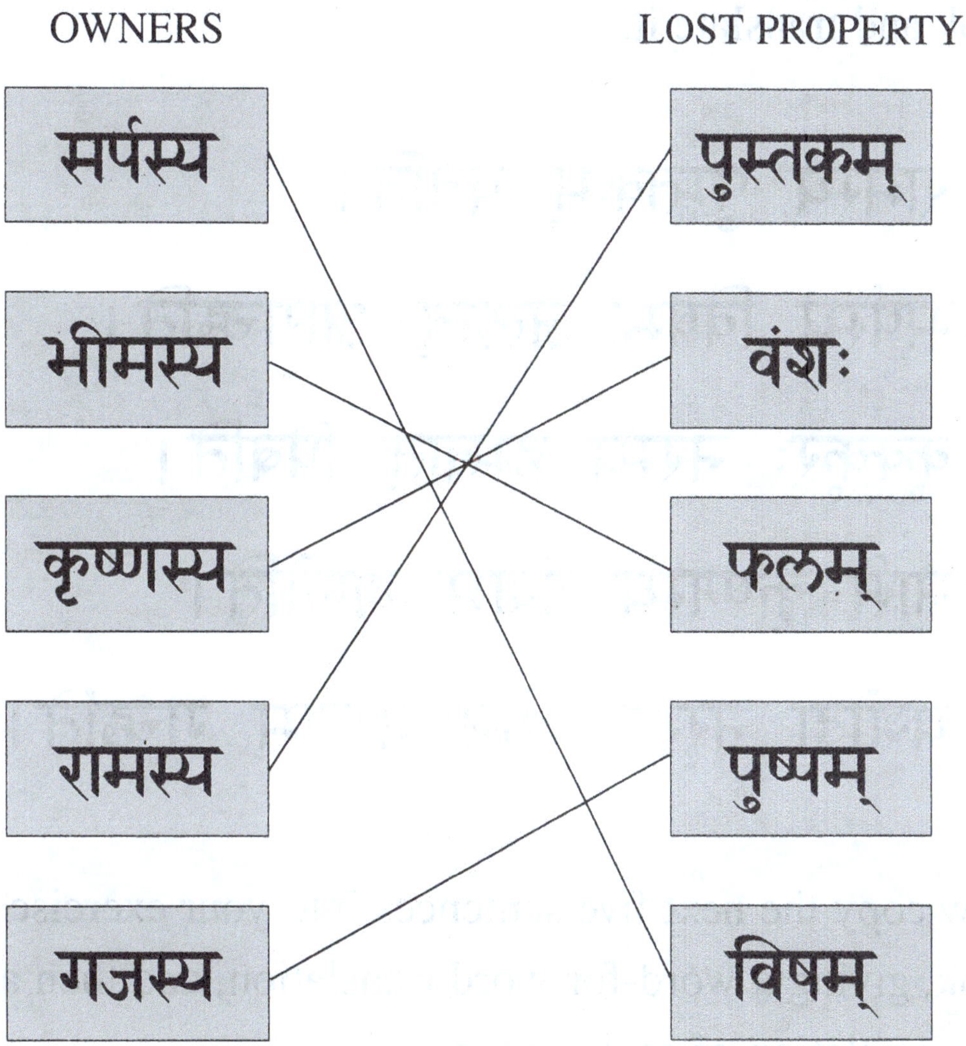

Find out who owns each piece of lost property by following the lines connecting the boxes. Write out who owns what in your exercise book like this:

रामस्य पुस्तकम् 'Rāma's book'

Exercise 13

Find a word with a Sixth Ending in each of the following five sentences, copy it into your exercise book and translate it.

1. रामस्य पुस्तकम् पतति।
2. सर्पस्य विषम् जलात् आगच्छति।
3. कुक्कुरः नरस्य हस्तात् पिबति।
4. नारी कृष्णस्य वंशम् शृणोति।
5. यशोदा नरस्य रथेन नगरम् गच्छति।

Now copy the next five sentences into your exercise book, giving a word-for-word translation, and then a full translation of each sentence.

6. नरस्य कुक्कुरात् धावति।

[continues next page →]

[continued]

7. कृष्णस्य वंशम् पश्यति।

8. रामस्य रथेन गच्छति।

9. कृष्णस्य गजात् पतति।

10. नरस्य हस्तात् पिबति।

Exercise 14

(a) Copy each of the following sentences beautifully into your exercise book.

(b) Underline

- ❖ the **verbs** in GREEN,
- ❖ the **First Ending** words in RED,
- ❖ the **Second Ending** words in BLUE,
- ❖ the **Third Ending** words in YELLOW,
- ❖ the **Fourth Ending** words in PINK,
- ❖ the **Fifth Ending** words in ORANGE, and
- ❖ the **Sixth Ending** words in BLACK.

(c) Give a word-for-word and then a full translation of each sentence.

1. विशालः गजः सिंहात् चरति।

2. सा दीर्घेण सूत्रेण कृष्णम् बध्नाति।

3. प्राज्ञः नरः गोविन्दाय नमति।

4. वीरः कृष्णः नगरात् रथेन गच्छति।

5. प्रबलः सर्पः कृष्णाय पुष्पम् ददाति।

6. हे नर रामस्य कुक्कुरः धावति।

STORY 2

Pūtanā Tries to Poison Kṛṣṇa

NEW WORDS:

पूतना	Pūtanā, a demoness	स्तनः	breast
		सस्मितम्	smilingly
राक्षसी	demoness	रक्तम्	blood
तस्याः	her	क्रोशति	cries out
उपरम	stop!	तु	but (always 2nd in a sentence)
मृत°	dead		

1. पूतना राक्षसी अस्ति।

2. सा कृष्णस्य गृहम् आगच्छति।

3. कृष्णः तस्याः स्तनात् पिबति।

[continues on page 33 →]

Kṛṣṇa overcomes Pūtanā.

[continued from page 31]

4. तत्र विषम् अस्ति।

5. सः विषम् सस्मितम् पिबति पिबति।

6. पूतना क्रोशति ‘हे कृष्ण उपरम उपरम’।

7. कृष्णः तु तस्याः रक्तम् सस्मितम् पिबति।

8. पूतना क्रोशति ‘हे कृष्ण उपरम उपरम’।

9. कृष्णः तु पिबति पिबति।

10. पूतना पतति।

11. सा मृता॥

[The teacher should find this story on page 56 of Volume 3 of the ‘Śrīmad Bhāgavatam’, translated by Swami Tapasyananda (1981), and fill in the details for the class.]

CHAPTER 4

The Seventh Ending

A noun can show where something is.
In English we say ***in***.

- The lady is ***in*** **the garden.**
- The boy is ***in*** **the classroom.**
- The king is ***in*** **the palace.**

Exercise 15

Copy these sentences into your exercise book, and underline in PURPLE the words that show ***where*** something is.

1. Flowers are growing in the garden.

2. There are many trees in the forest.

3. The man sees the fish in the river.

4. The girl swims every day in the sea.

5. They look at the stars shining in the sky.

In Sanskrit,
to say ***where***
something is we use
a special ending.

This is the
Seventh Ending.

The Seventh
Ending
means
'in'.

Exercise 16

Copy these sentences into your exercise book, and underline in PURPLE the words which would take the Seventh Ending in Sanskrit.

1. The soldier shows courage in the battle.

2. The girl finds her books in the playground.

3. The boy sees the mistake in the exercise book.

4. Yaśodā knows that Kṛṣṇa is in the house.

5. The gardens close in the winter.

The Seventh Ending is –ए.

So

रथः becomes रथे 'in the chariot'

and

हस्तः becomes हस्ते 'in the hand'.

Exercise 17

Read the three examples in the shaded box below and then copy them into your exercise book.

Examples:

वृक्षः	वृक्षे	in the tree
मत्स्यः	मत्स्ये	in the fish
सर्पः	सर्पे	in the snake

Exercise 18

(a) Copy into your exercise book the eight First Ending words given below, one below the other.

(b) Write beside them the same words with a Seventh Ending.

(c) Finally give the English meaning alongside each Seventh Ending word. The first question is done for you.

1.	रामः	रामे	in Rāma
2.	रथः		
3.	गजः		
4.	कालियः		
5.	सर्पः		
6.	सिंहः		
7.	वंशः		
8.	कुक्कुरः		

Exercise 19

Copy these, giving the English for each:

For example: खगः वृक्षे the bird in the tree

1. कृष्णः सर्पे
2. कुक्कुरः गृहे
3. सिंहः वने
4. नरः रथे
5. खगः हस्ते
6. रथः मार्गे
7. मत्स्यः जले
8. नरः चन्द्रे

Note: The Seventh Ending can sometimes mean 'on'.

For example:

नरः गजे अस्ति। The man is on the elephant.

❋ ❋ ❋

THE 'WHERE IS IT ?' GAME

Look at the picture on the next page.
Here is a list of six things in the picture:

1. गजः	**3.** सिंहः	**5.** पुष्पम्
2. नारी	**4.** रथः	**6.** खगः

In your exercise book, write six Sanskrit sentences saying ***where*** each thing is, and give the English for each sentence. The first one is done for you.

गजः अचले अस्ति। The elephant is on the mountain.

CHAPTER 5

The Forms of राम

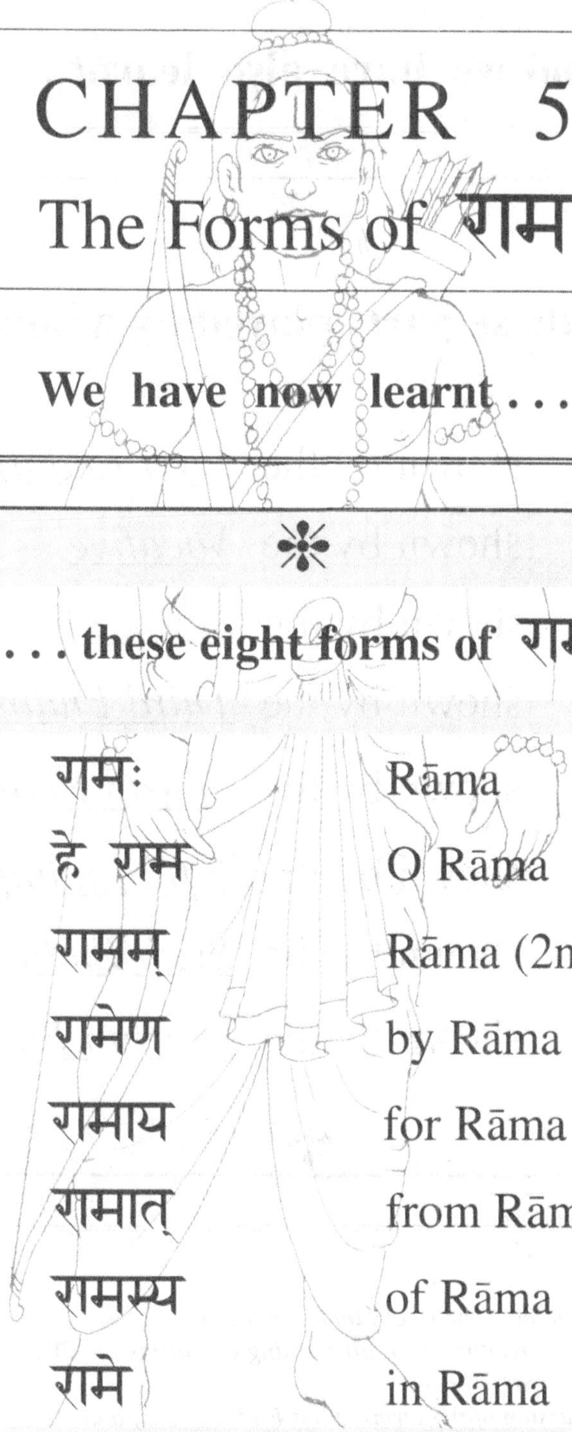

We have now learnt . . .

❋

. . . these eight forms of राम

रामः	Rāma
हे राम	O Rāma
रामम्	Rāma (2nd)
रामेण	by Rāma
रामाय	for Rāma
रामात्	from Rāma
रामस्य	of Rāma
रामे	in Rāma

❋

Practise reciting the above forms of राम *before moving on.*

And we have also learnt . . .

. . . these parts played by a noun:

doer	shown by the *First Ending*
called	shown by the *Vocative*
done to	shown by the *Second Ending*
by	shown by the *Third Ending*
for	shown by the *Fourth Ending*
from	shown by the *Fifth Ending*
of	shown by the *Sixth Ending*
in	shown by the *Seventh Ending*

During the next few weeks there should be:
(1) a daily recitation of all the singular forms of राम *shown on the preceding page;*
(2) discussion of the terms 'First Ending' etc., and
(3) practice in putting this knowledge into use.
The above list of the roles played should be learnt by heart and discussed.

Exercise 20

Copy these, giving the English for each:

For example: वृक्षे in the tree

1. रामे
2. रामस्य
3. रामात्
4. रामाय
5. हे राम
6. रामेण
7. रामम्
8. गजः
9. गजस्य
10. गजात्
11. हे गज
12. गजम्
13. खगे
14. खगेन
15. खगम्
16. खगस्य
17. नरे
18. नरात्
19. नरस्य
20. नराय

Exercise 21

In your exercise book, copy each Sanskrit sentence with its word-for-word translation and also with its complete translation. In each sentence **add the missing Sanskrit word**.

1. .... नरः आगच्छति ।

O Rāma the man comes

☞ O Rāma, the man comes.

2. सीता .... वदति ।

Sītā Rāma (2nd) speaks

☞ Sītā speaks to Rāma.

3. खगः .... गच्छति ।

The bird from Rāma goes

☞ The bird goes from Rāma.

4. नरः ………………………… वदति।

The man for Rāma speaks

☞ The man speaks for Rāma.

5. ………………………… कुक्कुरः खादति।

of Rāma dog eats

☞ Rāma's dog eats.

6. सीता सर्वम् ………………… पश्यति।

Sītā everything (2nd) in Rāma sees

☞ Sītā sees everything in Rāma.

7. ………………………… खादति।

Rāma eats

☞ Rāma eats.

STORY 3

The Demon Agha Swallows Kṛṣṇa

NEW WORDS:

अघः	Agha	तस्य	his
नाम	by name	धारयति	puts on
इव	like, as if	रूपम्	form
गुहा	cave	भवति	becomes

1. वने राक्षसः अघः नाम।

2. सः सर्पस्य रूपम् धारयति।

3. सः कृष्णम् गच्छति।

[*continues on page 50* →]

Kṛṣṇa and his friends enter the mouth of Agha.

[continued from page 48]

4. अघः कृष्णम् पश्यति।

5. तस्य आस्यम् गुहा इव भवति।

6. कृष्णः विशालाम् गुहाम् प्रविशति।

7. अघः कृष्णम् खादति।

8. सर्पे तु कृष्णः विशालः भवति।

9. सः अनन्तः अस्ति।

10. अघः मृतः भवति।

11. कृष्णः वनात् सस्मितम् गच्छति।

[See page 83 of Volume 3 of Swami Tapasyananda's translation of the 'Śrīmad Bhāgavatam' (1981 ed.).]

CHAPTER 6

The Forms of सीता

Creatures are created either

male or ***female***.

* man or woman *
* lion or lioness *
* god or goddess *

Exercise 22

Say whether the following are male or female:

For example: A king is male.

1. bull
2. cow
3. lion
4. lioness
5. father
6. mother
7. brother
8. sister
9. son
10. daughter

☞ Male words are called **masculine**.
☞ Female words are called **feminine**.

In Sanskrit,
masculine words
have endings
like रामः.

Feminine words in
Sanskrit have
different endings.

We will use
सीता as an example
of words with
feminine endings.

ENDINGS FOR FEMININE WORDS

Here are the first four forms of सीता.

These forms should be practised regularly until well known.

सीता	Sītā
हे सीते	O Sītā
सीताम्	Sītā (2nd)
सीतया	by Sītā

Exercise 23

Copy these, giving the English for each:

For example: सीतया by Sītā

1. सीता
2. हे सीते
3. सीतया
4. सीताम्
5. नौका
6. नौकाम्
7. हे नौके
8. नौकया
9. तारका
10. तारकाम्
11. तारकया
12. यशोदा
13. हे यशोदे
14. यशोदाम्
15. यशोदया
16. नासिका
17. हे नासिके
18. नासिकाम्
19. नासिकया
20. हे तारके

Exercise 24

Copy these, giving the Sanskrit for each:

For example: Sītā सीता

1. Sītā
2. Sītā (2nd)
3. by Sītā
4. O Sītā
5. O star
6. star (2nd)
7. by a star
8. by Rāma
9. in Rāma
10. from Rāma
11. for Rāma
12. O Rāma
13. Rāma
14. Rāma (2nd)
15. of Rāma
16. for Rāma
17. for an elephant
18. in an elephant
19. in a bird
20. by Yaśodā

Exercise 25

For each of the following sentences:

(a) Copy it beautifully into your exercise book.

(b) Write a translation below each word.

(c) Give a full translation of the sentence.

> **For example:**
>
> यशोदा नौकाम् धावति ।
>
> Yaśodā | boat (2nd) | runs
>
> Yaśodā runs to the boat.

1. रामः नौकया गच्छति ।
2. रामः सीताम् चरति ।
3. सीता तारकाम् पश्यति ।
4. हे यशोदे सीता कृष्णस्य नासिकाम् पश्यति ।
5. नौका यशोदाम् आगच्छति ।

[The following exercise is for faster pupils only.]

Exercise 26

Copy into your exercise book these sentences. For each give a Sanskrit word-for-word translation, and then give a translation with correct Sanskrit word order. For example:

Rāma	goes	by boat.
रामः	गच्छति	नौकया ।

रामः नौकया गच्छति ।

1. Sītā sees the lion's nose.

2. The boat comes to Kṛṣṇa.

3. Bhīma runs to Rāma's boat.

4. The elephant walks to Sītā.

ENDINGS FOR FEMININE WORDS

Here are four more forms of सीता.

These forms should be practised regularly until well known.

सीतायै	for Sītā
सीतायाः	from Sītā
सीतायाः	of Sītā
सीतायाम्	in Sītā

We now know the first eight forms of मीता

मीता	Sītā
हे मीते	O Sītā
मीताम्	Sītā (2nd)
मीतया	by Sītā
मीतायै	for Sītā
मीतायाः	from Sītā
मीतायाः	of Sītā
मीतायाम्	in Sītā

Practise reciting the above forms of मीता *before moving on to Exercise 27, and thereafter practise them regularly.*

Exercise 27

Copy these, giving the English for each:

For example:	सीतायै	for Sītā

1. सीतायाम्
2. सीतायाः (give 2 answers)
3. सीतायै
4. सीता
5. हे सीते
6. सीताम्
7. सीतया
8. तारका
9. तारकायै
10. तारकायाम्
11. तारकायाः (give 2 answers)
12. तारकाम्
13. हे तारके
14. नौका
15. नौकायाम्
16. नौकायाः (give 2 answers)
17. नौकायै
18. नौकाम्
19. यशोदायाम्
20. यशोदायै

Exercise 28

Copy these, giving the Sanskrit for each:

For example: of Sītā सीतायाः

1.	in Sītā	**11.**	for Rāma
2.	for Sītā	**12.**	from a star
3.	from Sītā	**13.**	by a star
4.	of Sītā	**14.**	in a boat
5.	by Sītā	**15.**	from a boat
6.	O Sītā	**16.**	of a boat
7.	Sītā (2nd)	**17.**	by a boat
8.	from Sītā	**18.**	in Yaśodā
9.	in a star	**19.**	from Yaśodā
10.	for a star	**20.**	of Yaśodā

Exercise 29

Copy these, giving the English for each:

1. रामात्
2. सीतायै
3. सीतायाम्
4. रामस्य
5. सीतायाः (give 2 answers)
6. गजे
7. नौकायाम्
8. खगस्य
9. यशोदायाः (give 2 answers)
10. तारकायाम्

Exercise 30

Copy these, giving the Sanskrit for each:

1. by Yaśodā
2. for Sītā
3. in an elephant
4. by chariot
5. by Sītā
6. in a star
7. for a bird
8. from the boat
9. O Sītā
10. Rāma (2nd)

[The following exercise is for faster pupils only.]

Exercise 31

Copy these English sentences. For each give a Sanskrit word-for-word translation, and then give a translation with correct Sanskrit word order. For example:

Rāma	sees	Sītā (2nd).
रामः	पश्यति	सीताम् ।

रामः सीताम् पश्यति ।

1. Sītā sees Rāma (2nd).
2. Rāma goes by chariot.
3. Sītā goes to Rāma.
4. Sītā jumps from the tree.
5. Rāma's dog runs to the boat.

CHAPTER 7

The Forms of मित्रम्

So far we have had masculine or feminine words. Some words in Sanskrit are ***neither masculine nor feminine:*** they are called *'**neuter**'*.

Exercise 32

The Sanskrit words for these are all neuter. You already know them. Copy these English words, giving the Sanskrit for each:

For example: town नगरम्

1. friend

2. forest

3. rope

4. book

5. butter

6. chair

7. mouth

8. water

9. chin

10. door

11. everything

12. flower

13. fruit

14. house

15. town

16. heart

The word
'neuter'
means
'neither masculine
nor feminine'.

In Sanskrit, neuter
words have
endings like those
of मित्रम् 'friend'.

We shall use मित्रम्
as an example
of words with
neuter endings.

Here are the first eight forms of मित्रम्

मित्रम्	friend
हे मित्र	O friend
मित्रम्	friend (2nd)
मित्रेण	by a friend
मित्राय	for a friend
मित्रात्	from a friend
मित्रस्य	of a friend
मित्रे	in a friend

These forms are to be practised regularly, and examples of the forms of other neuter words should be demonstrated by the teacher.

Exercise 33

Write out the first eight forms of मित्रम् and of वनम्. (Remember that there is न, not ण, in the ending of वनेन because there is no र in that word.)

Exercise 34

Copy these, giving the English for each:

1. मित्रेण
2. मित्रस्य
3. मित्रात्
4. मित्रम् (give 2 answers)
5. मित्रे
6. मित्राय
7. हे मित्र
8. सूत्रम् (give 2 answers)
9. सूत्रात्
10. सूत्रेण
11. रामे
12. रामाय
13. सीताम्
14. सीतया
15. तारकायाः (give 2 answers)
16. वनम् (give 2 answers)
17. वनेन
18. नासिकायै
19. सिंहात्
20. राक्षसम्
21. खगाय
22. गुहायै
23. नौकायाम्
24. सीतायै

Exercise 35

Copy these, giving the Sanskrit for each:

1. by a friend
2. for a friend
3. from a friend
4. O friend
5. in a friend
6. friend (2nd)
7. of a friend
8. in a forest
9. by a forest
10. for a forest
11. from a forest
12. by a rope
13. in a rope
14. of a rope
15. rope (2nd)
16. rope
17. in Sītā
18. by Sītā
19. for Rāma
20. of Rāma

Exercise 36

For each of the following sentences:

(a) Copy it beautifully into your exercise book.

(b) Write a translation below each word.

(c) Give a full translation of the sentence.

For example:

फलम्	हरितात्	वृक्षात्	पतति।
fruit	from green	from the tree	falls

The fruit falls from the green tree.

1. सः राक्षसस्य रूपम् धारयति।
2. राक्षसी विशालाम् गुहाम् प्रविशति।
3. अघः दीर्घः सर्पः भवति।
4. कुक्कुरः वृक्षात् प्लवनम् करोति।
5. नरः सीतायै नमति।

STORY 4

The Whirlwind Demon

NEW WORDS:

चक्रवातः	whirlwind	गृहीत॰	grabbed
गगनम्	sky	भूम्याम्	on the ground
नयति	leads		
क्षिपति	throws	हत॰	killed
कण्ठः	throat		

1. राक्षसः चक्रवातस्य रूपे अस्ति।

2. सः कृष्णम् आगच्छति।

3. कृष्णः चक्रवातेन गृहीतः अस्ति।

[*continues on page 74* →]

Kṛṣṇa grabs the Whirlwind Demon's throat.

[continued from page 72]

4. यशोदा क्रोशति।

5. चक्रवातः कृष्णम् गगने नयति।

6. कृष्णेन राक्षसस्य कण्ठः गृहीतः अस्ति।

7. कृष्णः राक्षसम् गगनात् क्षिपति।

8. राक्षसः भूम्याम् पतति।

9. राक्षसः हतः अस्ति।

10. कृष्णः राक्षसे सस्मितम् उपविशति॥

[See page 62 of Volume 3 of Swami Tapasyananda's translation of the 'Śrīmad Bhāgavatam' (1981 ed.).]

CHAPTER 8

The Dual – 'Speaking of Two'

The Sanskrit scriptures say that everything is One. In language, however, we speak of this One showing itself as ***one***, ***two*** or ***many***.

In English, when we speak of two or more things, we add an 's'. So 'cat' becomes 'cats'. In Sanskrit, we add special endings when we speak of ***two*** or of ***many*** .

So far we know only endings for speaking of **ONE** thing.

This is called '**SINGULAR**'.

Now we shall learn the endings for speaking of **TWO** things.

These endings are called '**DUAL**'.

To speak of 'two Rāmas' we say रामौ.

गजौ means 'two elephants'

and

खगौ means 'two birds'.

THE नौका GAME

There is a flood. Two of each type of creature enter a boat. They are kept in the boat until the flood is over. Here are pictures of some of the creatures that enter the boat in pairs. In your exercise book write the dual form for each picture, together with its translation.

Example 1.	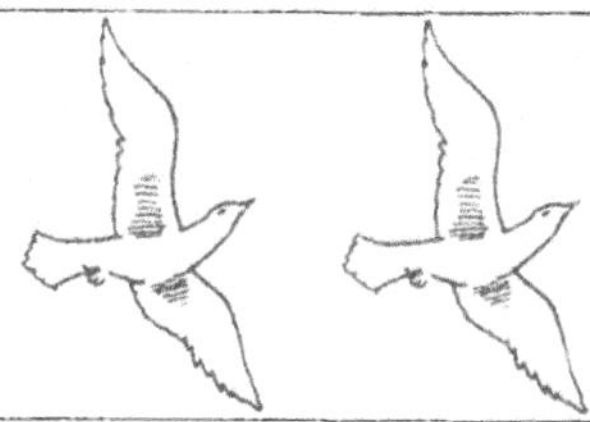	खगौ two birds

2. 

3. 

4.

5.

We shall now put the dual forms of राम next to the singular forms that we have already practised.

रामः	*Rāma*	रामौ	*two Rāmas*
हे राम	*O Rāma*	हे रामौ	*O two Rāmas*
रामम्	*Rāma* (2nd)	रामौ	*two Rāmas* (2nd)
रामेण	*by Rāma*	रामाभ्याम्	*by two Rāmas*
रामाय	*for Rāma*	रामाभ्याम्	*for two Rāmas*
रामात्	*from Rāma*	रामाभ्याम्	*from two Rāmas*
रामस्य	*of Rāma*	रामयोः	*of two Rāmas*
रामे	*in Rāma*	रामयोः	*in two Rāmas*

Practise reciting the above forms of राम, ***reading across,*** *before moving on to Exercise 37.*

Exercise 37

1. Copy out the dual forms of राम with their meanings.
2. Now do the same for all the dual forms of गज beginning with गजौ ('two elephants').

As you can see on the previous page, in the dual forms of राम

1st Vocative 2nd	forms always end in – औ
3rd 4th 5th	forms always end in – आभ्याम्
6th 7th	forms always end in – अयोः

Exercise 38

Give all the possible English meanings for:

1. रामौ
2. रामाभ्याम्
3. रामयोः
4. गजौ
5. गजाभ्याम्
6. गजयोः
7. खगौ
8. खगयोः
9. खगाभ्याम्
10. नरौ

Exercise 39

Give the Sanskrit for:

1. by two Rāmas
2. in two Rāmas
3. two Rāmas
4. O two Rāmas
5. for two Rāmas
6. of two Rāmas
7. from two Rāmas
8. two Rāmas (2nd)
9. two birds
10. by two birds
11. in two birds
12. from two birds

Exercise 40

Give all the possible English meanings for:

1.	रामौ	**6.**	रामाय
2.	रामात्	**7.**	सीतया
3.	रामाभ्याम्	**8.**	गजाभ्याम्
4.	रामे	**9.**	गजयोः
5.	रामयोः	**10.**	सीतायाम्

Exercise 41

Give the Sanskrit for:

1.	two Rāmas	**7.**	of a bird
2.	in Rāma	**8.**	in two birds
3.	of Rāma	**9.**	of Sītā
4.	of two Rāmas	**10.**	in Sītā
5.	in two Rāmas	**11.**	in two birds
6.	in an elephant	**12.**	from two birds

We shall now put the dual forms of सीता next to the singular forms that we have already practised.

सीता	*Sītā*	सीते	*two Sītās*
हे सीते	*O Sītā*	हे सीते	*O two Sītās*
सीताम्	*Sītā* (2nd)	सीते	*two Sītās* (2nd)
सीतया	*by Sītā*	सीताभ्याम्	*by two Sītās*
सीतायै	*for Sītā*	सीताभ्याम्	*for two Sītās*
सीतायाः	*from Sītā*	सीताभ्याम्	*from two Sītās*
सीतायाः	*of Sītā*	सीतयोः	*of two Sītās*
सीतायाम्	*in Sītā*	सीतयोः	*in two Sītās*

Practise reciting the above forms of सीता, *reading across, before moving on to Exercise 42.*

Exercise 42

Give all the possible English meanings for:

1. सीते
2. सीताभ्याम्
3. सीतयोः
4. सीतया
5. सीताम्
6. तारके
7. गजाय
8. तारकयोः
9. नासिकाभ्याम्
10. नौकयोः

Exercise 43

Translate into Sanskrit:

1. two Sītās (2nd)
2. by two Sītās
3. of two Sītās
4. two Sītās
5. from two Sītās
6. in two Sītās
7. O two Sītās
8. for two Sītās
9. two stars
10. in two stars
11. from two stars
12. two stars (2nd)

We shall now put the dual forms of मित्रम् next to the singular forms.

मित्रम्	*friend*	मित्रे	*two friends*
हे मित्र	*O friend*	हे मित्रे	*O two friends*
मित्रम्	*friend* (2nd)	मित्रे	*two friends* (2nd)
मित्रेण	*by a friend*	मित्राभ्याम्	*by two friends*
मित्राय	*for a friend*	मित्राभ्याम्	*for two friends*
मित्रात्	*from a friend*	मित्राभ्याम्	*from two friends*
मित्रस्य	*of a friend*	मित्रयोः	*of two friends*
मित्रे	*in a friend*	मित्रयोः	*in two friends*

Practise reciting the above forms of मित्रम्, *reading across, before moving on to Exercise 44.*

Notice that मित्रम् is the same as राम except in the First, Vocative and Second Endings.

Exercise 44

Give all the possible English meanings for:

1.	मित्रे	**6.**	वने
2.	मित्रयोः	**7.**	पुष्पे
3.	मित्राभ्याम्	**8.**	पुष्पाभ्याम्
4.	वनयोः	**9.**	पुष्पयोः
5.	वनाभ्याम्	**10.**	रूपाभ्याम्

Exercise 45

Translate into Sanskrit:

1.	two friends	**6.**	O two friends
2.	by two friends	**7.**	for two friends
3.	in two friends	**8.**	of two friends
4.	from two friends	**9.**	two forests
5.	two friends (2nd)	**10.**	two flowers

Exercise 46

Translate into Sanskrit:

1. from two Sītās
2. in two lions
3. of two Sītās
4. O two birds
5. by two friends
6. in two friends
7. of two elephants
8. two snakes
9. by two dogs
10. two forms

VERBS SPEAKING OF TWO

We have seen that a **NOUN** has a **dual** ending when we speak of **two** things. So also a **VERB** has its own **dual** ending when **two** people or things do something.

For example:

भवति he, she or it becomes	भवतः they two become

In the same way:

पतति he, she or it falls	पततः they two fall

NOTE: भवति can mean :

‘**<u>he</u>**	becomes’
‘**<u>she</u>**	becomes’
or	
‘**<u>it</u>**	becomes’

In the same way, पतति can mean:

‘**<u>he</u>**	falls’
‘**<u>she</u>**	falls’
or	
‘**<u>it</u>**	falls’

Exercise 47

Translate into English, giving all possible meanings:

1. भवति
2. भवतः
3. पतति
4. पततः
5. खादति
6. खादतः
7. नमति
8. नमतः
9. वदतः
10. वदति

Exercise 48

Translate into Sanskrit:

1. he becomes
2. it falls
3. they two become
4. they two fall
5. they two eat
6. she eats
7. he bows
8. they two speak
9. she speaks
10. they two bow

Notice that when **TWO** people
do something,
both the noun and the verb
have DUAL endings.

For example:

खगौ खादतः । The two birds eat.

Exercise 49

Translate into English:

1. वृक्षौ पततः ।
2. वृक्षः पतति ।
3. नरौ पश्यतः ।
4. नरः पश्यति ।
5. मित्रे वदतः ।
6. मित्रम् वदति ।
7. पुस्तकम् पतति ।
8. पुस्तके पततः ।
9. नरौ अनन्तौ भवतः ।
10. नरः अनन्तः भवति ।

Exercise 50

Translate into Sanskrit:

1. Two trees fall.
2. Two men eat.
3. Two friends speak.
4. A friend falls.
5. Two birds fall.
6. A man becomes limitless..
7. Two men become limitless.
8. Two birds eat.

STORY 5

Kṛṣṇa Releases the Sons of Kubera

NEW WORDS:

कुबेरः	Kubera, god of wealth	कुपित°	angry
पुत्रः	son	उलूखलम्	large bowl
गर्वित°	proud	मध्ये	in the middle
स्तः	they two are	छिन्न°	cut
नारदः	Nārada, a great sage	अन्तः	inside
शप्त°	cursed	पुरुषः	person
शापः	curse	मुक्त°	freed
एकदा	once		

1. कुबेरस्य पुत्रौ गर्वितौ स्तः।

2. पुत्रौ नारदेन शप्तौ भवतः।

[continues on page 95 →]

Kṛṣṇa releases the sons of Kubera.

[continued from page 93]

3. पुत्रौ शापेन वृक्षौ प्रविशतः।

4. एकदा कृष्णेन नवनीतम् गृहीतम् अस्ति।

5. यशोदा कुपिता भवति।

6. सा कृष्णम् उलूखले बध्नाति।

7. सः वृक्षयोः मध्ये गच्छति।

8. उलूखलेन वृक्षौ छिन्नौ भवतः।

9. वृक्षौ पततः।

10. वृक्षयोः अन्तः पुरुषौ स्तः।

11. पुरुषौ कुबेरस्य पुत्रौ स्तः।

12. कृष्णेन पुत्रौ मुक्तौ भवतः॥

[See page 73 of Volume 3 of Swami Tapasyananda's translation of the 'Śrīmad Bhāgavatam' (1981 ed.).]

CHAPTER 9

The Plural – 'Speaking of Many'

We have seen how in Sanskrit
we add some endings called
'singular' when we speak of ***one*** thing,
and other endings called 'dual' when we speak
of ***two*** things. Now we shall learn endings
called 'plural' for speaking of
more than two things.

We shall show the plural by saying 'many'.

To speak of 'many Rāmas'
we say रामाः.
गजाः means 'many elephants'
and
खगाः means 'many birds'.

We shall now put the plural forms of राम next to the singular and dual forms that we have already practised.

रामः	*Rāma*	रामौ	*two Rāmas*	रामाः	*many Rāmas*
हे राम	*O Rāma*	हे रामौ	*O two Rāmas*	हे रामाः	*O many Rāmas*
रामम्	*Rāma* (2nd)	रामौ	*two Rāmas* (2nd)	रामान्	*many Rāmas* (2nd)
रामेण	*by Rāma*	रामाभ्याम्	*by two Rāmas*	रामैः	*by many Rāmas*
रामाय	*for Rāma*	रामाभ्याम्	*for two Rāmas*	रामेभ्यः	*for many Rāmas*
रामात्	*from Rāma*	रामाभ्याम्	*from two Rāmas*	रामेभ्यः	*from many Rāmas*
रामस्य	*of Rāma*	रामयोः	*of two Rāmas*	रामाणाम्	*of many Rāmas*
रामे	*in Rāma*	रामयोः	*in two Rāmas*	रामेषु	*in many Rāmas*

Practise reciting the above forms of राम *before starting Exercise 52.*

Exercise 51

(a) Copy out all the forms of राम beautifully into your exercise book as shown in the table.
(b) Now do the same for गज, with English translations.
(c) Finally do the same for खग, but with no translations.

Exercise 52

Translate into English, giving all possible meanings:

1. रामाः
2. रामान्
3. हे रामाः
4. रामैः
5. रामेभ्यः
6. रामाणाम्
7. रामेषु
8. गजान्
9. गजैः
10. गजेभ्यः
11. गजानाम्
12. गजेषु
13. खगान्
14. खगैः
15. खगेभ्यः

Exercise 53

Translate into Sanskrit:

1. for many Rāmas
2. in many Rāmas
3. from many Rāmas
4. of many Rāmas
5. O many Rāmas
6. many Rāmas
7. by many Rāmas
8. many Rāmas (2nd)
9. many elephants (2nd)
10. O many elephants
11. from many birds
12. by many elephants
13. for many elephants
14. in many elephants
15. of many elephants

Exercise 54

Translate into English, giving all possible meanings:

1. रामाः
2. रामे
3. रामौ
4. हे राम
5. हे रामाः
6. हे रामौ
7. रामान्
8. रामैः
9. रामेषु
10. रामात्
11. रामस्य
12. रामाणाम्
13. रामाभ्याम्
14. रामयोः
15. रामाय

Exercise 55

Translate into Sanskrit:

1. for Rāma
2. of Rāma
3. in two Rāmas
4. by many Rāmas
5. in Rāma
6. by two Rāmas
7. of many Rāmas
8. for two Rāmas
9. O Rāma
10. O many Rāmas

VERBS SPEAKING OF MANY

When we speak of **<u>many</u>** people or things doing something, we use another ending.

For example:

भवन्ति 'they many become'

So we have:

भवति he, she or it becomes	भवतः they two become	भवन्ति they many become

In the same way:

खादति he, she or it eats	खादतः they two eat	खादन्ति they many eat
चरति he, she or it walks	चरतः they two walk	चरन्ति they many walk

Exercise 56

Copy the following table into your exercise book, filling in the gaps.

SINGULAR	DUAL	PLURAL
भवति he, she or it becomes	भवतः they two become	भवन्ति they many become
चरति he, she or it walks		
खादति he, she or it eats		
गच्छति he, she or it goes		
पश्यति he, she or it sees		
प्रविशति he, she or it enters		

Note:

अस्ति he, she or it is	स्तः they two are	सन्ति they many are

Exercise 57

Translate into English:

1. नमति	7. हसति
2. नमतः	8. हसन्ति
3. नमन्ति	9. हसतः
4. धावन्ति	10. अस्ति
5. धावतः	11. स्तः
6. धावति	12. सन्ति

Exercise 58

Translate into Sanskrit:

1. she bows

2. they many bow

3. they two bow

4. he laughs

5. they two laugh

6. they many laugh

7. she is

8. they many are

9. they two are

10. they many run

Notice that when **MANY** people do something, both the noun and the verb have PLURAL endings.

For example:

नराः खादन्ति

Exercise 59

Translate into English:

1. खगाः पतन्ति।
2. नराः हसन्ति।
3. सिंहाः प्रविशन्ति।
4. गजाः पिबन्ति।
5. मत्स्याः गच्छन्ति।
6. सिंहाः पतन्ति।
7. मत्स्यौ गच्छतः।
8. नरौ खादतः।
9. मित्रे पिबतः।
10. नौके गच्छतः।

च 'and'

In Sanskrit, 'च' comes **after** the two words being put together.

For example:

सीता यशोदा च

Sītā and Yaśodā

Exercise 60

Translate into English:

1. गजः सिंहः च
2. नरः कुक्कुराः च
3. खगाः मत्स्याः च
4. रामः सीता च
5. सिंहः सर्पः च

STORY 6

Brahmā Hides the Cowherd Boys and the Calves

NEW WORDS:

गोपालः	cowherd	पितामहः	the Creator
वत्सः	calf	पुनः	again
दूरे	far away	न कुत्र चित्	nowhere
तिरोहित°	hidden	नव°	new

1. कृष्णः गोपालाः च वने खादन्ति ।

2. गोपालानाम् वत्साः दूरे चरन्ति ।

3. पितामहेन वत्साः तिरोहिताः सन्ति ।

[continues on page 111 →]

Brahmā hides the cowherd boys and the calves.

[continued from page 109]

4. कृष्णः वत्सान् न कुत्र चित् पश्यति।

5. पितामहेन गोपालाः तिरोहिताः सन्ति।

6. कृष्णः गोपालान् न कुत्र चित् पश्यति।

7. सः नवान् गोपालान् करोति।

8. सः नवान् वत्सान् करोति।

9. पितामहः नवान् वत्सान् पश्यति।

10. पितामहः नवान् गोपालान् पश्यति।

11. पितामहः कृष्णाय नमति।

12. तिरोहिताः वत्साः पुनः आगच्छन्ति।

13. तिरोहिताः गोपालाः पुनः आगच्छन्ति॥

[See page 88 of Volume 3 of Swami Tapasyananda's translation of the 'Śrīmad Bhāgavatam' (1981 ed.).]

Exercise 61

(a) Copy out beautifully into your exercise book all the forms of मीता as shown on the next page, but without their translations.

(b) Now do the same for नौका.

(c) Finally do the same for तारका.

We shall now put the plural forms of सीता next to the singular and dual forms that we have already practised.

सीता	*Sītā*	सीते	*two Sītās*	सीताः	*many Sītās*
हे सीते	*O Sītā*	हे सीते	*O two Sītās*	हे सीताः	*O many Sītās*
सीताम्	*Sītā* (2nd)	सीते	*two Sītās* (2nd)	सीताः	*many Sītās* (2nd)
सीतया	*by Sītā*	सीताभ्याम्	*by two Sītās*	सीताभिः	*by many Sītās*
सीतायै	*for Sītā*	सीताभ्याम्	*for two Sītās*	सीताभ्यः	*for many Sītās*
सीतायाः	*from Sītā*	सीताभ्याम्	*from two Sītās*	सीताभ्यः	*from many Sītās*
सीतायाः	*of Sītā*	सीतयोः	*of two Sītās*	सीतानाम्	*of many Sītās*
सीतायाम्	*in Sītā*	सीतयोः	*in two Sītās*	सीतासु	*in many Sītās*

Practise reciting the above forms of सीता *before starting Exercise 62.*

Exercise 62

Translate into English, giving all possible meanings:

1. सीताः
2. हे सीताः
3. सीताभिः
4. सीताभ्यः
5. सीतानाम्
6. सीतासु
7. सीताम्
8. सीतया
9. सीते
10. हे सीते
11. सीतायाः
12. सीताभ्याम्
13. सीतयोः
14. सीतायै
15. सीतायाम्
16. नौकाः
17. नौकासु
18. नासिकानाम्
19. नासिकाभ्यः
20. नासिकाः

Exercise 63

Translate into Sanskrit:

1. in many Sītās
2. by many Sītās
3. for many Sītās
4. many Sītās (2nd)
5. many Sītās
6. of many Sītās
7. O Sītā
8. by Sītā
9. by two Sītās
10. in two Sītās
11. from Sītā
12. in many boats
13. in two boats
14. by a boat
15. in a boat
16. from the boats
17. many boats (2nd)
18. by many boats
19. from a boat
20. of the boat

Exercise 64

Translate into English, giving all possible meanings:

1. रामः	11. सीते
2. रामात्	12. सीतयोः
3. रामे	13. सीताः
4. रामौ	14. सीतासु
5. रामाभ्याम्	15. रामाय
6. रामाः	16. सीतानाम्
7. रामेषु	17. रामाणाम्
8. सीता	18. रामेभ्यः
9. सीताम्	19. सीताभ्यः
10. सीतायाम्	20. रामस्य

Exercise 65

Translate into Sanskrit:

1. by Rāma
2. in Rāma
3. two Rāmas
4. many Rāmas
5. O Rāma
6. Sītā
7. by Sītā
8. for Sītā
9. by two Sītās
10. in many Sītās
11. in many Rāmas
12. by many Rāmas
13. for many Rāmas
14. from many Rāmas
15. by two Rāmas
16. in two Sītās
17. for two Sītās
18. O Sītā
19. from many Sītās
20. of many Sītās

Exercise 66

Translate into English, giving all possible meanings:

1. रामाः
2. खगाः
3. सीताः
4. नौकाः
5. रामेषु
6. सीतासु
7. नौकासु
8. गजेषु
9. गजेभ्यः
10. नौकाभ्यः

We shall now put the plural forms of **मित्रम्** next to the singular and dual forms that we have already practised.

मित्रम्	*friend*	मित्रे	*two friends*	मित्राणि	*many friends*
हे मित्र	*O friend*	हे मित्रे	*O two friends*	हे मित्राणि	*O many friends*
मित्रम्	*friend* (2nd)	मित्रे	*two friends* (2nd)	मित्राणि	*many friends* (2nd)
मित्रेण	*by a friend*	मित्राभ्याम्	*by two friends*	मित्रैः	*by many friends*
मित्राय	*for a friend*	मित्राभ्याम्	*for two friends*	मित्रेभ्यः	*for many friends*
मित्रात्	*from a friend*	मित्राभ्याम्	*from two friends*	मित्रेभ्यः	*from many friends*
मित्रस्य	*of a friend*	मित्रयोः	*of two friends*	मित्राणाम्	*of many friends*
मित्रे	*in a friend*	मित्रयोः	*in two friends*	मित्रेषु	*in many friends*

Practise reciting the above forms of मित्रम् *before moving on to Exercise 67.*

Exercise 67

Give all possible English translations of the following:

1.	मित्रम्	6.	हे मित्र
2.	मित्रेण	7.	मित्रे
3.	मित्राय	8.	मित्रेषु
4.	मित्रैः	9.	मित्राणाम्
5.	मित्राणि	10.	मित्रेभ्यः

Exercise 68

Translate into Sanskrit:

1.	many friends	**6.**	for many friends
2.	by many friends	**7.**	by a friend
3.	in many friends	**8.**	from a friend
4.	from many friends	**9.**	from two friends
5.	of many friends	**10.**	in a friend

Exercise 69

Give all possible English translations of the following:

1. पुष्पम्
2. पुष्पाणि
3. पुष्पे
4. पुष्पाय
5. नगरे
6. नगराभ्याम्
7. नगरैः
8. द्वारे
9. द्वाराणि
10. द्वारात्

Exercise 70

Give the Sanskrit for:

1. two friends
2. two flowers
3. many friends
4. many flowers
5. many towns
6. of many doors
7. in many doors
8. from many towns
9. by two doors
10. O friends

CHAPTER 10

Person

The Sanskrit scriptures say that there is only one Person. In language, however, we speak of this one Person in three ways:

- When we say 'he, she or it becomes' we could be speaking about anyone or anything. In Sanskrit, **'he, she or it'** are called the **FIRST PERSON**.
- When we say 'you become' we are speaking to the person in front of us. In Sanskrit, **'you'** is called the **MIDDLE PERSON.**
- When we say 'I become' we are speaking about the person within. In Sanskrit, **'I'** is called the **BEST PERSON**.

Exercise 71

Copy each of these sentences into your exercise books, and say whether it is the FIRST, MIDDLE or BEST PERSON.

For example: I walk. BEST PERSON

1. She becomes.
2. You become.
3. I become.
4. They two become.
5. They many become.
6. He runs.
7. I run.
8. You run.
9. They two run.
10. They many run.
11. You fall.
12. They two fall.
13. I fall.
14. They many fall.
15. You bow.
16. He bows.
17. I give.
18. You give.
19. She gives.
20. They two are.

THE FIRST PERSON

So we have seen the FIRST PERSON in

the singular: **'he, she or it'**
the dual: **'they two'**
and
the plural: **'they many'**

In Sanskrit, the endings for the FIRST PERSON are –ति, – तः and – न्ति:
For example:

भवति	भवतः	भवन्ति
he/she/it becomes	**they two become**	**they many becom**

Exercise 72

Copy the following table into your exercise book, filling in the gaps:

SINGULAR	DUAL	PLURAL
भवति he/she/it becomes	भवतः they two become	भवन्ति they many become
गच्छति he/she/it goes	गच्छतः they two go	गच्छन्ति they many go
चरति he/she/it walks	.... ________	.... ________
पश्यति	.... ________	.... ________
प्रविशति	.... ________	.... ________
खादति	.... ________	.... ________

We have seen that the FIRST PERSON is 'he', 'she' or 'it', 'they two' or 'they many'.

So we say गच्छति 'he, she or it goes', गच्छतः 'they two go' and गच्छन्ति 'they many go'.

Now we shall look at the MIDDLE and BEST PERSONS.

The MIDDLE PERSON is **'you'**.

In Sanskrit, the ending for the

MIDDLE PERSON is -असि.

For example:

भवसि	गच्छसि	खादसि
you become	**you go**	**you eat**

The BEST PERSON is **'I'**.

In Sanskrit, the ending for the

BEST PERSON is -आमि.

For example:

भवामि	गच्छामि	खादामि
I become	**I go**	**I eat**

Exercise 73

Give the English for:

1. भवति
2. भवतः
3. भवन्ति
4. भवसि
5. भवामि
6. गच्छति
7. गच्छतः
8. गच्छन्ति
9. गच्छसि
10. गच्छामि
11. पश्यति
12. पश्यसि
13. पश्यामि
14. धावति
15. धावसि
16. धावामि
17. खादति
18. खादामि
19. खादसि
20. पिबामि

Exercise 74

Give the Sanskrit for:

1. he goes
2. they two go
3. they many go
4. you go
5. I go
6. he sees
7. they two see
8. they many see
9. you see
10. I see
11. he eats
12. she eats
13. it eats
14. they two eat
15. they many eat
16. you eat
17. I eat
18. you run
19. I run
20. she sees

'You' can also be 'two' or 'many'. So we have

'you two' and **'you many'**

When the BEST PERSON is spoken of as 'two' or 'many' it becomes 'we'. So we have

'we two' and **'we many'**.

Just as the FIRST PERSON can be singular, dual or plural, so also can the MIDDLE and BEST PERSONS. In this way we have these nine forms of भवति.

	Singular	*Dual*	*Plural*
First Person	भवति he/she/it becomes	भवतः they two become	भवन्ति they many become
Middle Person	भवसि you become	भवथः you two become	भवथ you many become
Best Person	भवामि I become	भवावः we two become	भवामः we many become

Now begin to practise all the nine forms of भवति *shown above, reciting across line by line.*

Exercise 75

Give the English for:

1. भवति
2. भवतः
3. भवन्ति
4. भवसि
5. भवथः
6. भवथ
7. भवामि
8. भवावः
9. भवामः
10. भवथ

Exercise 76

Give the Sanskrit for:

1. he becomes
2. you become
3. I become
4. we two become
5. we many become
6. they two become
7. they many become
8. you two become
9. you many become
10. she becomes

Exercise 77

Give the English for:

1. पश्यति
2. पश्यतः
3. पश्यन्ति
4. पश्यसि
5. पश्यथः
6. पश्यथ
7. पश्यामि
8. पश्यावः
9. पश्यामः
10. गच्छामि
11. गच्छावः
12. गच्छथः
13. नमथः
14. पिबामि
15. पिबामः
16. खादावः
17. खादसि
18. खादन्ति
19. चरामः
20. चरथः

Exercise 78

Give the Sanskrit for:

1. she eats
2. they two eat
3. they many eat
4. I eat
5. we two eat
6. we many eat
7. you eat
8. you two eat
9. you many eat
10. I see
11. we two see
12. you two see
13. you many see
14. he sees
15. they many see
16. they two see
17. I bow
18. they two bow
19. they many bow
20. we two bow

Exercise 79

Give the English for:

1. सिंहः पश्यति।
2. सिंहम् पश्यति।
3. सिंहौ पश्यति।
4. सिंहान् पश्यति।
5. सिंहान् पश्यतः।
6. सिंहान् पश्यन्ति।
7. सिंहान् पश्यसि।
8. सिंहान् पश्यथः।
9. सिंहान् पश्यथ।
10. सिंहान् पश्यामि।

Exercise 80

Give the Sanskrit for:

1. He runs from the lion.
2. She runs from the lion.
3. They two run from the lion.
4. They two run from the two lions.
5. They many run from the two lions.
6. You run from the two lions.
7. You two run from the two lions.
8. You many run from the two lions.
9. I run from the two lions.
10. I run from the many lions.
11. We two run from the many lions.
12. We many run from the many lions.

Exercise 81

For each of the sentences on the next page:

(1) Write it in your exercise book.

(2) On the next line down, put a number showing which ending each noun has (for example, First – 1, Second – 2, Third – 3, and so on).

Do not write numbers underneath any adjectives, verbs or vocative words.

(3) Then give a word-for-word translation.

(4) On the last line, give a full translation.

For example:

हे राम	नरौ	वनात्	कृष्णाभ्याम्	गजाभ्याम्	गच्छतः ।
	1	5		3	
O Rāma	two men	from the forest	by two black	by two elephants	they two go
O Rāma, two men go from the forest by two black elephants.					

1. हे भीम अर्जुनः अरुणेन रथेन गच्छति।

2. यशोदा कृष्णम् सूत्रेण बध्नाति।

3. नरौ प्रबलान् सिंहान् पश्यतः।

4. गजाः वनात् धावन्ति।

5. कृष्णाय नमसि।

6. प्रबलात् सिंहात् धावामि।

7. रामाय नमथः।

8. गजेभ्यः पतथ।

9. वृक्षम् गच्छावः।

10. सर्पेभ्यः धावामः।

11. राक्षसस्य रथाः नगरम् गच्छन्ति।

12. वृक्षे खगौ खादतः।

CHAPTER 11

The Three Times

The Sanskrit scriptures say that there is only the Eternal. In language, however, we speak of this Eternal as existing in three times:

The time that has **gone** is the **Past.**
The time that is **now** is the **Present.**
The time that is **coming** is the **Future.**

Exercise 82

Copy each of these sentences into your exercise book, and say whether the verb is Past, Present or Future:

For example: 'He will go.' – **Future**

1. He eats.

2. He will eat.

3. She runs.

4. He will run.

5. She ran.

6. They two ran.

7. He sees.

8. She will see.

9. She saw.

10. They many bow.

11. They many will bow.

12. They many bowed.

The Future Time

So far we have used verbs speaking of the Present time, such as भवति.

When we speak of an action in the Future time, we add - इष्य before the ending.

So we have the form भविष्यति 'he, she or it will become'.

So we have:

	Singular	*Dual*	*Plural*
First Person	भविष्यति he, she or it will become	भविष्यतः they two will become	भविष्यन्ति they many will become
Middle Person	भविष्यसि you will become	भविष्यथः you two will become	भविष्यथ you many will become
Best Person	भविष्यामि I will become	भविष्यावः we two will become	भविष्यामः we many will become

Practise these Future forms of भवति *regularly until well established, reciting across, line by line. Also regularly recite the Present forms of* भवति.

Exercise 83

Give the English for:

1. भविष्यति
2. भविष्यतः
3. भविष्यन्ति
4. भविष्यसि

[continues on next page]

[continued]

5. भविष्यथः
6. भविष्यथ
7. भविष्यामि
8. भविष्यावः
9. भविष्यामः
10. भवति
11. भवामि
12. भवसि
13. भवतः
14. भवन्ति
15. भवावः
16. भवथ
17. भवथः
18. भवामः
19. भविष्यामि
20. भविष्यन्ति

Exercise 84

Give the Sanskrit for:

1. he will become
2. they many will become
3. I will become
4. we two will become
5. you will become
6. you many will become
7. we many will become
8. they two will become
9. you two will become
10. I become
11. she becomes
12. they many become
13. we many become

[continued on next page]

[continued]

14. we two become

15. you become

16. you many become

17. you two become

18. they two become

19. she will become

20. it will become

THE SPECIAL USE OF THE FIRST ENDING

In Sanskrit, when you **'become'** or **'are'** something, what you **'become'** or **'are'** takes the First Ending.

For example:

कृष्णः अनन्तः अस्ति । 'Kṛṣṇa is limitless.'

राक्षसः मृतः भवति । 'The demon becomes dead' or 'dies'.

Exercise 85

Give the English for:

1. मृताः भवन्ति।
2. मृताः भविष्यन्ति।
3. मित्रम् भवसि।
4. अनन्तौ भवथः।
5. मृताः भवथ।
6. अनन्तः अस्ति।
7. मृताः भविष्यामः।
8. कुपितः भविष्यति।
9. कुपितौ भविष्यावः।
10. कुपितौ भविष्यथः।

The Use of इति

In English, when you repeat exactly what someone else said or thought, you put speech marks <u>at the beginning and at the end</u> of their speech or thought. For example:

The king said: "Come here!"

[continued on next page →]

[continued]

In Sanskrit, when we repeat what someone else said or thought, we just put the word इति at the end of their speech or thought. For example:

मृतः भवामि इति वदति।	**"I am dying", he says.**

इति here is not translated as a separate word but as speech marks.

Exercise 86

Translate into English:

1. मृतः भवति इति वदति।

2. मृताः भवन्ति इति वदन्ति।

3. अनन्तौ भवथः इति वदति।

4. मृतः भविष्यति इति वदामि।

5. मृताः भविष्यन्ति इति वदति।

STORY 7

The Lifting of the Mountain

NEW WORDS:

इन्द्रः	Indra (the god who controls the rains)	मेघः	cloud
परमेश्वरः	the Supreme Lord	उद्धरति	lifts
इति	*see pages 145-6*	रक्षित॰	saved
वर्षाः	rains		

1. हे गोपालाः इन्द्रः न परमेश्वरः इति कृष्णः वदति।

2. इन्द्रः कुपितः भवति।

3. वर्षाः भविष्यन्ति इति इन्द्रः वदति।

[continues on page 149 →]

Kṛṣṇa lifts the mountain.

[continued from page 147]

4. मेघाः आगच्छन्ति।

5. वर्षाः पुनः पुनः पतन्ति।

6. मृताः भविष्यामः इति गोपालाः वदन्ति।

7. कृष्णः हस्तेन अचलम् उद्धरति।

8. गोपालाः कृष्णम् आगच्छन्ति।

9. गोपालाः वर्षेभ्यः रक्षिताः सन्ति।

10. इन्द्रः कृष्णाय नमति।

11. कृष्णस्य मित्रम् भविष्यामि इति इन्द्रः वदति॥

[See page 145 of Volume 3 of Swami Tapasyananda's translation of the 'Śrīmad Bhāgavatam' (1981 ed.).]

The Past Time

To form the Past time, we put अ before the verb, and use a special set of endings.

So, taking भवति, we first add an अ at the beginning, giving 'अभवति'.

Then we take the इ from the end, giving 'अभवत्' 'he, she or it became'.

So we have these nine Past endings:

	Singular	*Dual*	*Plural*
First Person	अभवत् he, she or it became	अभवताम् they two became	अभवन् they many became
Middle Person	अभवः you became	अभवतम् you two became	अभवत you many became
Best Person	अभवम् I became	अभवाव we two became	अभवाम we many became

Practise these Past forms of भवति *regularly until well established, reciting across, line by line. Also regularly recite the Present and Future forms (see pages 130 and 141).*

Exercise 87

Give the English for:

1. अभवत्
2. अभवताम्
3. अभवः
4. अभवन्
5. अभवतम्
6. अभवत
7. अभवम्
8. अभवाव
9. अभवाम
10. भवामि
11. भविष्यामि
12. भविष्यसि
13. भविष्यथः
14. भविष्यन्ति
15. भविष्यावः
16. भवामः
17. भवावः
18. भवति
19. भवसि
20. भवथः

Exercise 88

Translate into Sanskrit:

1. he became
2. you two became
3. I became
4. we many became
5. they many became
6. you became
7. we two became
8. you many became
9. they two became
10. I become
11. I will become
12. we two will become
13. they two become
14. she will become
15. they will become
16. we many will become
17. we many became
18. we two become
19. they many become
20. it becomes

Exercise 89

Give the English for:

1. अभवत्
2. अधावत्
3. अवदताम्
4. अवदन्
5. अधावन्
6. अपतत्
7. अपतत
8. अपतम्
9. अधावाव
10. अवदाम

STORY 8

The Wrestling Match

NEW WORDS:

कंसः	Kaṁsa (name of a wicked king)	मिलति	meets (with a word having a 3rd ending) e.g. गजेन मिलति 'he meets an elephant'
असाधुः	evil		
नृपः	king		
मम	my	भूमिम्	ground (2nd)
चाणूरः	Cāṇūra (name of a wrestler)	प्रति	towards (used after a word with a 2nd ending)
प्रबल०	powerful		
अचिरेण	soon	क्षिपति	throws

[Story begins on page 157 →]

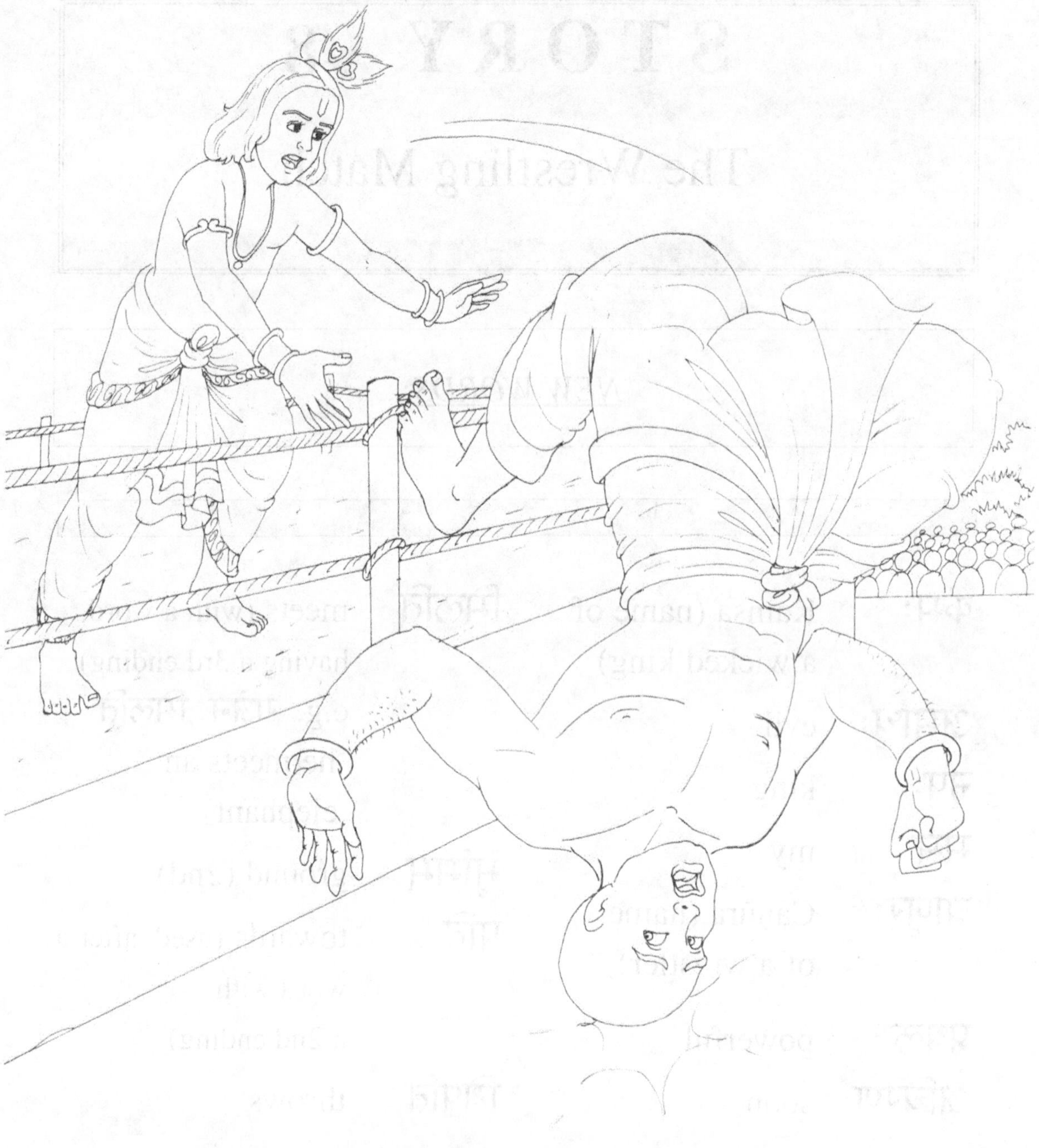

Kṛṣṇa defeats Cāṇūra.

[continued from page 155]

1. कंसः असाधुः नृपः अस्ति।
2. कृष्णः न मम मित्रम् इति कंसः अवदत्।
3. कंसस्य मित्रम् चाणूरः नाम।
4. चाणूरः प्रबलः नरः अस्ति।
5. अचिरेण कृष्णः युद्धे चाणूरेण अमिलत्।
6. चाणूरस्य हस्तः कृष्णेन गृहीतः अस्ति।
7. कृष्णः चाणूरम् भूमिम् प्रति अक्षिपत्।
8. चाणूरः मृतः अभवत्॥

[See page 213 of Volume 3 of Swami Tapasyananda's translation of the 'Śrīmad Bhāgavatam' (1981 ed.).]

CHAPTER 12

The Forms of अस्ति

Now we will begin
to look more closely at
the verb अस्ति.
The forms of अस्ति do **not** go
like भवति.

We will now learn these three forms of the First Person of अस्ति in the Present Time:

अस्ति he, she or it is	स्तः they two are	सन्ति they many are

Often अस्ति can also mean 'there is',
and स्तः or सन्ति can mean 'there are'.

For example:

खगः अस्ति।	There is a bird.
मित्रे स्तः।	There are two friends.
सिंहाः सन्ति।	There are many lions.

The **Past** Time of अस्ति is

आसीत्

which means 'he, she or it was' or 'there was'.

For example:

खगः कृष्णः आसीत् । The bird was black.

खगः आसीत् । There was a bird.

Exercise 90

Give the English for:

1. वृक्षः अस्ति।
2. वृक्षाः सन्ति।
3. खगौ स्तः।
4. खगाः सन्ति।
5. खगाः कृष्णाः सन्ति।
6. वृक्षाः हरिताः सन्ति।
7. खगौ हरितौ स्तः।
8. सिंहाः प्रबलाः सन्ति।
9. नरः प्रबलः आसीत्।
10. नरौ स्तः।

STORY 9

Kaṁsa's Destruction

<u>*NEW WORDS*</u>:

पीठम्	chair	अहो अहो	O my! O my!
आसीत्	was	जनः	person
व्यापादयति	kills	सर्वत्र	everywhere
प्लवनम्	a jump	आनन्दः	bliss
अकरोत्	made	जयति	is victorious
केशः	hair		

1. कंसः पीठे आसीत्।
2. सः चाणूरम् मृतम् अपश्यत्।

[continues on page 164 →]

Kṛṣṇa defeats Kaṁsa.

[continued from page 162]

3. अचिरेण कृष्णम् व्यापादयिष्यामि इति कंसः अवदत्।

4. कृष्णः कंसम् प्रति प्लवनम् अकरोत्।

5. कंसस्य केशाः कृष्णेन गृहीताः सन्ति।

6. कृष्णः कंसम् पीठात् भूमिम् प्रति अक्षिपत्।

7. कंसः मृतः अभवत्।

8. अहो अहो इति जनाः अक्रोशन्।

9. पुष्पाणि गगनात् अपतन्।

10. सर्वत्र आनन्दः आसीत्।

11. कृष्णः जयति॥

[See page 217 of Volume 3 of Swami Tapasyananda's translation of the 'Śrīmad Bhāgavatam' (1981 ed.).]

APPENDICES

1. **Verses to Recite**
2. **Lists of Word Forms**
3. **List of Words: English - Sanskrit**
4. **List of Words: Sanskrit - English**

APPENDIX 1

VERSES TO RECITE

*The following verses can be recited daily, section by section, progressing gradually until known by heart. The verses are taken from the **Bhagavad Gītā**, in which Kṛṣṇa advises Arjuna, who is about to engage in battle. Kṛṣṇa speaks as God incarnate, hence capital letters are used for 'My' and 'Me' etc.*

Chapter 12: Kṛṣṇa describes the man who is dear to Him.

अद्वेष्टा सर्वभूतानां मैत्रः करुण एव च ।
निर्ममो निरहंकारः समदुःखसुखः क्षमी ॥ 13 ॥

He who has hatred for none, ever friendly, compassionate, free from possession or pride, the same in pleasure and pain, in adversity patient ~

संतुष्टः सततं योगी यतात्मा दृढनिश्चयः ।
मय्यर्पितमनोबुद्धिर्यो मद्भक्तः स मे प्रियः ॥ 14 ॥

Who is always contented, united, controlled, with unshaken conviction, his reason and mind in My service, that man, so devoted to Me, I hold dear.

यस्मान्नोद्विजते लोको लोकान्नोद्विजते च यः।
हर्षामर्षभयोद्वेगैर्मुक्तो यः स मे प्रियः॥ 15 ॥

He who disturbs not the world, nor is disturbed by the world, free from pangs of excitement, impatience and fear, such a man I hold dear.

Chapter 13: Kṛṣṇa speaks of the one God in all creatures.

सर्वतः पाणिपादं तत् सर्वतोऽक्षिशिरोमुखम्।
सर्वतः श्रुतिमल्लोके सर्वमावृत्य तिष्ठति॥ 13 ॥

Everywhere It has hands and feet; everywhere It has eyes, heads and mouths; everywhere It is listening. It abides in the world, enveloping all.

सर्वेन्द्रियगुणाभासं सर्वेन्द्रियविवर्जितम्।
असक्तं सर्वभृच्चैव निर्गुणं गुणभोक्तृ च॥ 14 ॥

It shines through all workings of body, of senses and mind, yet is free of them all, detached yet upholding all things, beyond Nature's qualities, yet watching their play.

बहिरन्तश्च भूतानामचरं चरमेव च।
सूक्ष्मत्वात्तदविज्ञेयं दूरस्थं चान्तिके च तत् ॥ 15 ॥

Within all, outside all, unmoving yet moving, far away yet near, too subtle to be understood,

अविभक्तं च भूतेषु विभक्तमिव च स्थितम्।
भूतभर्तृ च तज्ज्ञेयं ग्रसिष्णु प्रभविष्णु च ॥ 16 ॥

In all beings undivided, yet appearing divided, That to be known is Supporter, Devourer and Origin too.

ज्योतिषामपि तज्ज्योतिस्तमसः परमुच्यते।
ज्ञानं ज्ञेयं ज्ञानगम्यं हृदि सर्वस्य विष्ठितम् ॥ 17 ॥

Light of all lights, beyond darkness, Knowledge, what needs to be known, goal of knowledge, It lives in the hearts of all.

APPENDIX 2
LISTS OF WORD FORMS

All the paradigms for nouns and verbs introduced in either Part One or Part Two of the 'Stories of Krishna' are reproduced in this appendix for easy reference.

The forms of भवति in the **Present** are:

	Singular	***Dual***	***Plural***
First Person	भवति he/she/it becomes	भवतः they two become	भवन्ति they many become
Middle Person	भवसि you become	भवथः you two become	भवथ you many become
Best Person	भवामि I become	भवावः we two become	भवामः we many become

The forms of भवति in the **Future** are:

	Singular	*Dual*	*Plural*
First Person	भविष्यति he, she or it will become	भविष्यतः they two will become	भविष्यन्ति they many will become
Middle Person	भविष्यसि you will become	भविष्यथः you two will become	भविष्यथ you many will become
Best Person	भविष्यामि I will become	भविष्यावः we two will become	भविष्यामः we many will become

The forms of भवति in the **Past** are:

	Singular	*Dual*	*Plural*
First Person	अभवत् he, she or it became	अभवताम् they two became	अभवन् they many became
Middle Person	अभवः you became	अभवतम् you two became	अभवत you many became
Best Person	अभवम् I became	अभवाव we two became	अभवाम we many became

The three forms of the First Person of अस्ति in the **Present** are:

अस्ति he, she or it is	स्तः they two are	सन्ति they many are

The **Past** Time of अस्ति is:

आसीत् 'he, she or it was' or 'there was'

The forms of राम

रामः	*Rāma*	रामौ	*two Rāmas*	रामाः	
हे राम	*O Rāma*	हे रामौ	*O two Rāmas*	हे रामाः	*O many R ¯mas*
रामम्	*Rāma* (2nd)	रामौ	*two Rāmas* (2nd)	रामान्	*many Rāmas* (2nd)
रामेण	*by Rāma*	रामाभ्याम्	*by two Rāmas*	रामैः	*by many Rāmas*
रामाय	*for Rāma*	रामाभ्याम्	*for two Rāmas*	रामेभ्यः	*for many Rāmas*
रामात्	*from Rāma*	रामाभ्याम्	*from two Rāmas*	रामेभ्यः	*from many Rāmas*
रामस्य	*of Rāma*	रामयोः	*of two Rāmas*	रामाणाम्	*of many Rāmas*
रामे	*in Rāma*	रामयोः	*in two Rāmas*	रामेषु	*in many Rāmas*

The forms of सीता

सीता	*Sītā*	सीते	*two Sītās*	सीताः	*many Sītās*
हे सीते	*O Sītā*	हे सीते	*O two Sītās*	हे सीताः	*O many Sītās*
सीताम्	*Sītā* (2nd)	सीते	*two Sītās* (2nd)	सीताः	*many Sītās* (2nd)
सीतया	*by Sītā*	सीताभ्याम्	*by two Sītās*	सीताभिः	*by many Sītās*
सीतायै	*for Sītā*	सीताभ्याम्	*for two Sītās*	सीताभ्यः	*for many Sītās*
सीतायाः	*from Sītā*	सीताभ्याम्	*from two Sītās*	सीताभ्यः	*from many Sītās*
सीतायाः	*of Sītā*	सीतयोः	*of two Sītās*	सीतानाम्	*of many Sītās*
सीतायाम्	*in Sītā*	सीतयोः	*in two Sītās*	सीतासु	*in many Sītās*

The forms of मित्रम्

मित्रम्	*friend*	मित्रे	*two friends*	मित्राणि	*many friends*
हे मित्र	*O friend*	हे मित्रे	*O two friends*	हे मित्राणि	*O many friends*
मित्रम्	*friend* (2nd)	मित्रे	*two friends* (2nd)	मित्राणि	*many friends* (2nd)
मित्रेण	*by a friend*	मित्राभ्याम्	*by two friends*	मित्रैः	*by many friends*
मित्राय	*for a friend*	मित्राभ्याम्	*for two friends*	मित्रेभ्यः	*for many friends*
मित्रात्	*from a friend*	मित्राभ्याम्	*from two friends*	मित्रेभ्यः	*from many friends*
मित्रस्य	*of a friend*	मित्रयोः	*of two friends*	मित्राणाम्	*of many friends*
मित्रे	*in a friend*	मित्रयोः	*in two friends*	मित्रेषु	*in many friends*

APPENDIX 3

List of Words: English - Sanskrit

This English-Sanskrit vocabulary comprises in alphabetical order appropriate English renderings of all the Sanskrit words used in the exercises, games and stories found in both Part One and Part Two.

• A •

again पुनः

Agha, name of a demon अघः

and च

angry कुपित°

anywhere कुत्र चित्

are – they two are, there are स्तः

– they many are, there are सन्ति

Arjuna अर्जुनः

as if, like इव

• B •

battle युद्धम्

becomes भवति

best उत्तम°

Bhīma भीमः

binds बध्नाति

bird खगः

black कृष्ण°

bliss आनन्दः

blood रक्तम्

blue नील°

boat नौका

book पुस्तकम्

bowl (large) उलूखलम्
bows नमति
brave वीर॰
breast स्तनः
but तु
butter नवनीतम्
by name नाम

• C •

Cakravāta, the Whirl-wind demon चक्रवातः
calf वत्सः
cave गुहा
Cāṇūra चाणूरः
chair पीठम्
chariot रथः
chin चिबुकम्
climbs आरोहति
closes (the eyes) निमिषति
cloud मेघः
colour वर्णः
comes आगच्छति
conquers, is victorious जयति
cowherd गोपालः
Creator, the पितामहः
cries out क्रोशति
(a) curse शापः
cursed शप्त॰
cut छिन्न॰

• D •

dead मृत॰
demon राक्षसः
demoness राक्षसी
does, makes करोति
dog कुक्कुरः
door द्वारम्
drinks पिबति

• E •

eats	खादति
elephant	गजः
enters	प्रविशति
everything	सर्वम्
everywhere	सर्वत्र
evil	असाधु॰

• F •

falls	पतति
far away	दूरे
fearless	अभय॰
fish	मत्स्यः
flower	पुष्पम्
flute	वंशः
forest	वनम्
form	रूपम्
freed	मुक्त॰
fruit	फलम्
friend	मित्रम्

• G •

gives	ददाति
goes	गच्छति
grabbed	गृहीत॰
green	हरित॰
ground	भूमिम् (2nd)
on the ground	भूम्याम्

• H •

hair	केशः
hand	हस्तः
he	सः
hears	शृणोति
heart	हृदयम्
her, of her	तस्याः
hidden	तिरोहित॰

his, of his तस्य
hits तुदति
house गृहम्

• I •

Indra इन्द्रः
inside अन्तः
is, there is अस्ति

• J •

jump प्लवनम्
jumps प्लवनम् करोति

• K •

Kaṁsa कंसः
Kāliya, a serpent demon कालियः
kills व्यापादयति
killed हत°
king नृपः
Kubera, the god of wealth कुबेरः
Kṛṣṇa कृष्णः

• L •

Lakṣmaṇa लक्ष्मणः
lady नारी
large विशाल°
large bowl उलूखलम्
laughs हसति
leads नयति
lifts उद्धरति
like, as if इव
limitless अनन्त°
lion सिंहः

long दीर्घ°
long ago पुरा
Lord, the गोविन्दः

M

made, did अकरोत्
makes, does करोति
man नरः
meets मिलति
(in the) middle मध्ये
moon चन्द्रः
mountain अचलः
mouth आस्यम्
my मम

N

name, by name नाम
Nārada, a sage नारदः
new नव°
nose नासिका
not न
nowhere न कुत्र चित्

O

O! हे
O my! अहो
orange नारङ्ग°

P

person पुरुषः, जनः
plays (an instrument) वादयति
poison विषम्
proud गर्वित°
pure शुद्ध°
powerful प्रबल°

puts on धारयति
Pūtanā, a demoness पूतना

• R •

rains वर्षाः
Rāma रामः
red अरुण°
river नदी
road मार्गः
rope सूत्रम्
runs धावति

• S •

saved रक्षित°
sees पश्यति
serpent demon कालियः
she सा
shines भाति
short ह्रस्व°
silent तूष्णीम्
Sītā सीता
sits down उपविशति
sky गगनम्
small अल्प°
(with a) smile सस्मितम्
snake सर्पः
son पुत्रः
soon अचिरेण
speaks वदति
speech marks इति
star तारका
stop! उपरम
stops उपरमति
strong प्रबल°
sun सूर्यः
Supreme Lord, the परमेश्वरः

• T •

there	तत्र
there is; is	अस्ति
they two are	स्तः
they many are	सन्ति
throat	कण्ठः
throws	क्षिपति
towards (used after a 2nd-ending word)	प्रति
town	नगरम्
tree	वृक्षः

• V •

(is) victorious	जयति

• W •

walks	चरति
was, there was	आसीत्
water	जलम्
what ?	किम्
Whirlwind demon, the	चक्रवातः
will become	भविष्यति
wise	प्राज्ञ॰
writes	लिखति

• Y •

Yaśodā	यशोदा
yellow	पीत॰

APPENDIX 4

List of Words: Sanskrit - English

The following vocabulary comprises all the Sanskrit words used in the exercises, games and stories found in both Part One and Part Two. It is set out in the order of the Sanskrit alphabet as shown immediately after the Notes for Teachers/Students early in each volume.

अ

अकरोत् made, did

अघः Agha, name of a demon

अचलः mountain

अचिरेण soon

अनन्त॰ limitless

अन्तः inside

अभय॰ fearless

अरुण॰ red

अर्जुनः Arjuna

अल्प॰ small

असाधु॰ evil

अस्ति is, there is

अहो O my!

आ

आगच्छति comes

आनन्दः bliss

आरोहति climbs

आसीत् was, there was

आस्यम् mouth

इ

इति = speech marks (see p. 145)

इन्द्रः Indra

इव like, as if

उ

उत्तम° best

उद्धरति lifts

उपरम stop!

उपरमति stops

उपविशति sits down

उलूखलम् large bowl

ए

एकदा once

क

कण्ठः throat

करोति does, makes

कंसः Kaṁsa

कालियः Kāliya, a serpent demon

किम् what?

कुक्कुरः dog

कुत्र चित् anywhere

कुपित° angry

कुबेरः Kubera, the god of wealth

कृष्ण° black

कृष्णः Kṛṣṇa

केशः hair

क्रोशति cries out

क्षिपति throws

ख

खगः bird

खादति eats

ग

गच्छति goes

गगनम् sky

गजः elephant

गर्वित॰ proud

गुहा cave

गृहम् house

गृहीत॰ grabbed

गोपालः cowherd

गोविन्दः the Lord

च

च and

चक्रवातः the Whirlwind demon

चन्द्रः moon

चरति walks

चाणूरः Cāṇūra

चिबुकम् chin

छ

छिन्न॰ cut

ज

जनः person

जयति conquers; is victorious

जलम् water

त

तत्र	there
तस्य	his
तस्याः	her, of her
तारका	star
तिरोहित°	hidden
तु	but
तुदति	hits
तूष्णीम्	silent

द

ददाति	gives
दीर्घ°	long
दूरे	far away
द्वारम्	door

ध

धारयति	puts on
धावति	runs

न

न	not
न कुत्र चित्	nowhere
नगरम्	town
नदी	river
नमति	bows
नयति	leads
नरः	man
नव°	new
नवनीतम्	butter
नाम	by name

नारङ्ग° orange

नारदः Nārada, a sage

नारी lady

नासिका nose

निमिषति closes the eyes

नील° blue

नृपः king

नौका boat

प

पतति falls

परमेश्वरः the Supreme Lord

पश्यति sees

पितामहः the Creator

पिबति drinks

पीत° yellow

पीठम chair

पुनः again

पुरा long ago

पुरुषः person

पुष्पम् flower

पुस्तकम् book

पुत्रः son

पूतना Pūtanā, a demoness

प्रति (used after a 2nd-ending word) towards

प्रबल° strong

प्रविशति enters

प्राज्ञ° wise

प्लवनम् a jump

फ

फलम् fruit

ब

बध्नाति	binds

भ

भवति	becomes
भविष्यति	will become
भाति	shines
भीमः	Bhīma
भूमिम्	ground (2nd)
भूम्याम्	on the ground

म

मत्स्यः	fish
मध्ये	in the middle
मम	my
मार्गः	road
मित्रम्	friend
मिलति	meets
मुक्त°	freed
मृत°	dead
मेघः	cloud

य

यशोदा	Yaśodā
युद्धम्	battle

र

रक्तम	blood
रक्षित°	saved

रथः	chariot
राक्षसः	demon
राक्षसी	demoness
रामः	Rāma
रूपम्	form

ल

लक्ष्मणः	Lakṣmaṇa
लिखति	writes

व

वत्सः	calf
वदति	speaks
वनम्	forest
वर्णः	colour
वर्षाः	rains
वंशः	flute
वादयति	plays (an instrument)
विषम्	poison
विशाल°	large
वीर°	brave
वृक्षः	tree
व्यापादयति	kills

श

शप्त°	cursed
शापः	a curse
शुद्ध°	pure
शृणोति	hears

स

सन्ति	they many are; there are

सर्पः	snake
सर्वत्र	everywhere
सर्वम्	everything
सः	he
सस्मितम्	with a smile
सा	she
सिंहः	lion
सीता	Sītā
सूत्रम्	rope
सूर्यः	sun
स्तनः	breast
स्तः	they two are; there are

ह

हत॰	killed
हरित॰	green
हसति	laughs
हस्तः	hand
हृदयम्	heart
हे	O!
ह्रस्व॰	short